Haunt Your House For Halloween

Decorating Tricks & Party Treats

Cindy Fuller

Sterling Publishing Co., Inc. New York

A Sterling / Chapelle Book

Chapelle:
- ♥ Jo Packham, Owner
- ♥ Cathy Sexton, Editor
- ♥ Pauline Locke, Illustrator
- ♥ Staff: Marie Barber, Malissa Boatwright, Kass Burchett, Rebecca Christensen, Marilyn Goff, Michael Hannah, Amber Hansen, Shirley Heslop, Holly Hollingsworth, Susan Jorgensen, Susan Laws, Barbara Milburn, Ginger Mikkelsen, Linda Orton, Karmen Quinney, Leslie Ridenour, and Cindy Stoeckl

Designers:
- ♥ Holly Fuller
- ♥ Kelly Henderson
- ♥ Jamie Pierce
- ♥ Cindy Rooks

Photography:
- ♥ Kevin Dilley, Photographer for Hazen Photography
- ♥ Susan Laws, Jo Packham, and Cindy Rooks, Photo Stylists for Chapelle

A special thanks to Linda Durbano, Jo Packham, and Helena Watson for the use of their homes and to Lyle Dabb of Dabb's Produce for the use of pumpkins and cornstalks.

Thank you to the following companies for the use of their products: Delta Paints, Plaid Paints, Offray Ribbon, and Kunin Felt

If you have any questions or comments or would like information on specialty products featured in this book, please contact Chapelle, Ltd., Inc., P.O. Box 9252, Ogden, UT 84409 • (801) 621-2777 • (801) 621-2788 Fax

10 9 8 7 6 5 4 3 2 1

Paperback edition published in 2001 by
Sterling Publishing Company, Inc.
387 Park Avenue South, New York, NY 10016
© 1997 by Chapelle Ltd.
Distributed in Canada by Sterling Publishing
c/o Canadian Manda Group, One Atlantic Avenue, Suite 105
Toronto, Ontario, Canada M6K 3E7
Distributed in Great Britain and Europe by Chris Lloyd at Orca Book
Services, Stanley House, Fleets Lane, Poole BH15 3AJ, England.
Distributed in Australia by Capricorn Link (Australia) Pty. Ltd.
P.O. Box 704, Windsor, NSW 2756 Australia
Printed in China
All Rights Reserved

Sterling ISBN 0-8069-3567-7

Contents

General Instructions

Transferring Patterns for Cutting Wood or Metal:

* Pine or balsa
* Galvanized metal
* Transfer paper
* Pencil

Instructions:

* Enlarge or reduce appropriate pattern(s) as necessary.
* Place transfer paper, graphite side down, on pine, balsa, or metal and trace around outside edges of pattern with a pencil.

Cutting Wood Out:

* Jigsaw
* Craft knife

Instructions:

* Using a jigsaw, cut around pencil lines that have been traced onto pine.
* When using balsa, a sharp craft knife should be used to cut around pencil lines.

Sanding:

* Sandpaper

Instructions:

* When sanding is necessary, sandpaper should be used to smooth rough edges. Coarse-grit, medium-grit, and/or fine-grit sandpapers can be used.

Sealing Wood:

* Paintbrush, flat
* Gesso
* Primer/sealer

Instructions:

* Using a flat brush, seal wood for indoor use by applying a generous coat of gesso to all unfinished pine or balsa surfaces. Allow gesso to dry thoroughly before applying acrylic paints.
* Using a flat brush, seal wood for outdoor use by applying a generous coat of primer/sealer to all unfinished pine or balsa surfaces. Allow primer/sealer to dry thoroughly before applying acrylic paints.

Transferring Patterns for Detail Painting:

* Transfer paper
* Pencil

Instructions:

* Use the same pattern(s) used to cut wood out.
* Place transfer paper, graphite side down, on pine or balsa that has been base-coated with acrylic paint. Trace around all detail painting lines with a pencil. When transferring detail painting lines onto pine or balsa that has been base-coated with a dark acrylic paint color, use white transfer paper.

Painting Techniques:

* Paintbrushes, flat
* Paintbrushes, round
* Stipple brushes
* Cosmetic sponges
* Old toothbrushes
* Liner brushes

Instructions:

* **Base coating:** Flat brushes are generally used for applying base coats of acrylic paint. The size of paintbrush needed depends on the surface area to be covered. When painting small pieces of pine or balsa, a 1/4" flat brush is recommended. When painting large pieces of pine or balsa, a 1/2" to 1" flat brush is recommended. Apply one or two coats of acrylic paint to fronts, backs, and all outside edges of pine or balsa for full, opaque coverage. Allow base coats to dry thoroughly between each application and before detail painting.
* **Dry brushing:** Flat brushes or round brushes are used for dry brushing. Load a brush with a small

amount of acrylic paint, then wipe it on a paper towel until there is very little paint left in the bristles. Hold the brush in a vertical position and apply the paint using a circular motion moving from the center to the outside. The color will soften toward the outer edges. Allow paint to dry thoroughly.

✳ Float shading and Float highlighting: Flat brushes are used for float shading and float highlighting. The size of paintbrush needed depends on the desired width of the shading or highlighting. Dampen the brush, then wipe it on a paper towel until there is very little water left in the bristles. Load one corner of the brush with acrylic paint and stroke the brush back and forth on a palette to work the paint into the bristles and soften the color. Apply the brush to the painting surface. The paint color should appear darkest at the loaded corner and

gradually fade to clear water on the opposite corner. If the paint spreads all the way across the chisel edge of the bristles, rinse the brush and re-load. Allow paint to dry thoroughly.

✳ Fly specking: Fly specking is done with an old toothbrush. Dip the toothbrush in water, then shake it to remove excess water. Dip the bristles of the toothbrush into acrylic paint that has been slightly diluted with water. Hold the toothbrush about 6 to 8 inches away, with the bristles pointed toward the project. Draw a finger or thumb across the bristles toward you causing the paint to spatter onto the painted project. The size of the "fly specks" depends on the amount of water used to dilute the paint — more water results in larger specks; less water results in smaller specks.

✳ Linework: Linework is generally done with liner brushes and acrylic paint, but fine-point permanent markers can be used. Vary the size of the tip on the marker depending on the effect desired. Various

colored paints or inks can be used. When using permanent markers for linework, a matte spray varnish must be used to seal the paint. Other types of varnish will cause the ink to run.

✳ Sponge painting: Cosmetic sponges, new or worn out, are used for sponge painting. This painting technique is similar to stippling; it is a way to apply acrylic paint by repeated small touches. Dip the sponge in paint and wipe it on a paper towel to remove excess paint. Pounce the sponge up and down to apply paint to the painting surface. The more paint on the sponge, the more solid the effect. Less paint on the sponge produces a soft, light effect. It is

better to use less paint and apply several coats. Allow paint to dry thoroughly between each application.

✳ Stippling: Stipple brushes are used for stippling. This painting technique is simply a way to apply acrylic paint by repeated small touches. Load the brush with paint and wipe it on a paper towel to remove excess paint. Hold the brush in a vertical position. Pounce it up and down to apply paint to the painting surface. The more paint in the brush, the more solid the effect. Less paint in the brush produces a soft, light effect. It is better to use less paint and apply several coats. Allow paint to dry thoroughly between each application.

✳ Washing: Flat brushes are used for washing. This technique refers to the application of acrylic paint to a surface for transparent coverage. Mix the paint with water in a 1:3 ratio (25% paint to 75% water). Several coats of a light wash produce a soft, transparent color. Allow wash to dry thoroughly between each application.

Safety Tips

Dowel Setting:

* Crows
* Wooden dowels
* Drill with drill bits
* Wood glue

Instructions:

* When a crow is desired on a project, such as a fence, and it is obvious that hot glue will not hold the crow in position, dowel setting should be done.

* Drill holes the size of the diameter of the wooden dowels into the bottom of the crow and into the project where the crow is to sit.

* Cut the wooden dowel to an appropriate length and insert it into the drilled holes. Use wood glue to secure.

Choosing the Perfect Costume:

* Design costumes so children can walk easily, without tripping or falling.

* Make or buy costumes big enough that warm clothing can be worn underneath.

* Use light-colored fabrics or reflective tape so trick-or-treaters are visible at night.

* Outfit children in comfortable, well-fitting shoes. Over-sized shoes, such as mom's high-heels, contribute to sore feet, falls, spilled treats, and tears.

* Recommend face painting instead of wearing masks; masks make it difficult to see and breathe.

Before Setting Out:

* Plan and discuss the route trick-or-treaters will follow.

* Send a flashlight to help children see better and be seen more clearly.

* Do not allow children to travel alone or unsupervised — young children should be accompanied by an adult or responsible older child.

* Remind youngsters to use good manners and be courteous.

* Give children an early meal or a nutritious snack before they go out.

Rules Never To Be Broken:

* Instruct children to go only into familiar neighborhoods and choose well-lighted streets.

* Instruct children to avoid dark houses.

* Instruct children to walk — running from house to house can be dangerous.

* Instruct children to stay on sidewalks and out of the street. If there are no sidewalks, walk facing traffic.

* Instruct children to cross streets at intersections or crosswalks.

* Instruct children to avoid running out between parked cars and to watch for cars entering or exiting driveways.

* Instruct children not to cross lawns where unseen objects or the uneven terrain itself can present tripping hazards.

* Instruct children not to eat any candy or treats before they return home and have parents inspect them.

Bat Wings & Broomsticks

Floating Phantom

Photo on page 7.

Materials & Tools:
- ◆ Floral wire, 12"
- ◆ String, 1 yard
- ◆ Styrofoam ball, 6"
- ◆ Button, white, 1³/₄"
- ◆ Cotton fabric, white, 2 yards
- ◆ Fabric scissors
- ◆ Spray webbing, 1 can black, 1 can peach
- ◆ Craft glue
- ◆ Craft scissors
- ◆ Craft foam, black

Instructions:

1. Make a small loop in one end of floral wire. Tie one end of string to loop in floral wire.

2. Push floral wire through Styrofoam ball so string runs through ball. Untie string from wire loop.

3. Thread string through holes in button. Re-tie string to loop in floral wire.

4. Push floral wire back through Styrofoam ball so string runs back through ball. Untie string from wire loop and discard floral wire. Both ends of string should be coming out from top of Styrofoam ball and is anchored in by button on bottom of Styrofoam ball. Tie ends of string together to make a loop for hanging.

5. Fold cotton fabric in half vertically, then in half horizontally. On folded corner, cut off a small triangle to make a small hole in the center of the piece of fabric. Unfold fabric.

6. Spray top of Styrofoam ball and cotton fabric with black and peach spray webbing.

7. Drape fabric over Styrofoam ball and pull string loop through hole. Using craft glue, secure fabric onto Styrofoam ball.

8. Using Face pattern on page 94, cut two eyes and one mouth from black craft foam with craft scissors and glue on ghost as desired.

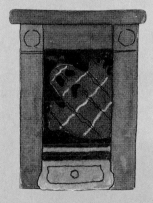

Great Bags of Fire

Photo on page 7.

Materials & Tools for each bag:
- ♥ Paper bags, any color, 6" wide x 11" high
- ♥ Cardboard, 5¹/₂" x 11"
- ♥ Pencil
- ♥ Graphite paper
- ♥ Craft knife
- ♥ Sand
- ♥ Votive candle

Instructions:

1. Place cardboard inside paper bag. Make certain folded sides are behind cardboard so they cannot be cut.

2. Using a pencil and graphite paper, trace desired pattern onto seamless side of paper bag. See Great Bags of Fire patterns on pages 79-80.

3. Using a craft knife, carefully cut the pattern from the bag. Make certain not to cut through the cardboard.

4. Place about 2" of sand in the bottom of each bag.

5. Place a votive candle in the center of each bag, using sand to anchor candle in place.

Pumpkin Posts

Photo on page 7.

Materials & Tools for each post:
- ◆ Firring strips, 2" x 2" x 3' with one pointed end
- ◆ Interior/exterior spackling compound
- ◆ Table knife
- ◆ Paintbrushes, flat
- ◆ Paintbrushes, round
- ◆ Acrylic paint colors: brown, green, orange
- ◆ Matte acrylic spray

Instructions:

1. Mix spackling compound with orange acrylic paint to desired shade.

2. Using a table knife, spread colored spackling compound onto all four sides of posts. Allow spackling compound to dry overnight.

3. Using a flat brush, paint tops of posts (about five or six inches) on all four sides with green.

4. Using a round brush, paint pumpkin faces on posts with brown.

5. Seal paint with matte acrylic spray.

Caught In A Web

Photo on page 7.

Materials & Tools:
- ♥ Plastic spider garland, 3½ yards
- ♥ Fabric scissors
- ♥ Fabric, Halloween print, ⅓ yard
- ♥ Hot glue gun and glue sticks
- ♥ Raffia: black, orange
- ♥ String
- ♥ Decorative accessories
- ♥ Craft foam: black, green, orange, white
- ♥ Craft glue

Instructions:

1. Using fabric scissors, cut Halloween-print fabric into three 4"-wide strips.

2. Using a hot glue gun and glue sticks, hot-glue each 4"-wide strip together, end to end, to make one 135"-long strip.

3. Fold 135"-long strip in half lengthwise and hot-glue together to make one 2"-wide, 135"-long strip.

4. Twist plastic spider garland and 135"-long fabric strip together and set aside.

5. Make characters to hang from garland and, using string, make a loop for hanging. Attach characters and additional decorative accessories to the garland by threading black and orange raffia through the string loops and tie in a bow.

6. To make pumpkins, use Pumpkin pattern on page 89 and cut one solid pumpkin and both strips from orange craft foam. Cut eyes and mouth from black craft foam and pumpkin stem from green craft foam. Using craft glue, adhere strips, eyes, mouth, and pumpkin stem in position on top of solid pumpkin.

7. To make bats, use Spooks' Night Out pattern on page 81 and cut one solid bat and two additional wings from black craft foam. Using craft glue, adhere bat wings on top of solid bat.

8. To make ghosts, use Spooks' Night Out pattern on page 81 and cut ghosts from white craft foam.

Face Painting

Unlike conventional masks, painting faces does not obscure a child's vision or breathing. It's safe, fun, and easy to do!

Mix 3 tablespoons corn starch to 1 tablespoon flour. Gradually stir in ¾ cup light corn syrup and ¼ cup water. Set aside ¼ cup of mixture. Divide the remaining mixture into small cups adding ½ teaspoon food coloring for each color desired.

- Mix red and yellow to make orange.
- Mix red and green to make black.

1. Apply the untinted mixture on child's face, avoiding all areas around the eyes.

2. Cover with one-ply white tissue paper and apply more untinted mixture. Let dry for 15 minutes.

3. Use tinted mixtures to do detail painting. To wash off, simply use a mild soap with warm water.

Try making a tiger using orange and black, a devil using red and black, or a clown using several colors!

Patch Work Prowler

Photo on page 8.

Materials & Tools:
✦ Styrofoam ball, 4"
✦ Styrofoam cone, 12"
✦ Hot glue gun and glue sticks
✦ Twigs, 7" (2)
✦ Fabric stiffener
✦ Cotton fabric, white, 3/4 yard
✦ Pinking shears
✦ Fabric scraps
✦ Craft glue
✦ Fabric paint, black

Instructions:
1. Using a hot glue gun and glue sticks, hot-glue Styrofoam ball to top of Styrofoam cone.

2. Push twigs into sides of cone approximately three to four inches from the top.

3. Using fabric stiffener, prepare white cotton fabric according to manufacturer's directions.

4. Place fabric over Styrofoam and twig ghost form. Arrange and position fabric as desired. Allow to dry for several hours.

5. Using pinking shears, cut fabric scraps into patches. Using craft glue, adhere patches to ghost as desired.

6. Using black fabric paint, draw ghost's eyes and draw stitches around fabric patches.

Jaw Breakers

Photo on page 8.

Materials & Tools:
✦ Wooden eggs, 3" (approximately 12); 5" (approximately 3)
✦ Gesso
✦ Paintbrushes, flat
✦ Acrylic paint colors: orange, white, yellow
✦ Matte acrylic spray
✦ Permanent marker, black
✦ Plastic cauldron, black
✦ Shredded paper or tissue paper
✦ Assorted ribbons

Instructions:
1. Seal wooden eggs with gesso.

2. Using a flat brush, paint wooden eggs to resemble candy corn: bottoms with yellow, centers with orange, tops with white.

3. Seal paint with matte acrylic spray.

4. Using a permanent black marker, write sayings on wooden candy corn as desired.

5. Fill plastic cauldron with shredded paper, tissue paper, or as desired and fill with wooden candy corn.

6. Using an assortment of ribbons, tie a bow around cauldron.

Going Batty

Photo on page 8.

Materials & Tools for each bat:
♥ Wire coat hanger
♥ Pliers
♥ Old pair pantyhose, black
♥ Craft scissors
♥ Black quilting thread
♥ Craft glue
♥ Rhinestones, assorted
♥ Fishing line

Instructions:
1. Using pliers, bend wire coat hanger into the shape of a bat.

2. Using craft scissors, cut one leg from an old pair of black pantyhose. Pull nylon over shaped bat — wing, center, wing. Fold remaining nylon back to center.

3. Wrap center of bat along both sides of body with black quilting thread until the desired shape is formed.

4. Using craft glue, adhere rhinestones to nylon as desired.

5. Use fishing line to hang bats in windows or from trees.

Ghoulish Delights

Photo on page 9.

Materials & Tools:
- ✦ Straw wreath, 14" diameter
- ✦ Assorted fabrics
- ✦ Pinking shears
- ✦ Individually-wrapped suckers (approximately 50)
- ✦ 1/8" ribbon: black, orange, natural
- ✦ Permanent markers: black, white
- ✦ Assorted ribbons, 4 yards each color
- ✦ Floral wire

Instructions:

1. Using pinking shears, cut assorted fabrics into 8½"-diameter circles. Cut one fabric circle for each sucker.

2. Place one sucker in center of each fabric circle and pull fabric up over sucker and around sucker stick. Tie 1/8" ribbons in a bow to secure fabric around sucker stick. Repeat for each sucker.

3. Using a permanent black or white marker, draw eyes and a nose on each ghost.

4. Push sucker sticks into straw wreath as desired until wreath is covered with ghosts.

5. Tie a bow with an assortment of ribbons and secure with wire to top, center of wreath.

6. Hang wreath on the front door so "trick-or-treaters" can pull the ghost of their choice from the hanging wreath!

Superstitions
- Wearing red on Halloween scares ghosts away.
- Wearing garlic on Halloween keeps vampires away.
- If the salt shaker falls, quickly throw some salt over your left shoulder to bring back good luck.
- If a cat jumps in your lap, good luck is on its way.
- Never rock an empty rocking chair — it will bring bad luck.

Fright Light

Photo on page 10.

Materials & Tools for each hurricane lamp:
- ♥ Clay saucer, 5" diameter
- ♥ Paintbrushes, flat
- ♥ Acrylic paint colors: black, purple
- ♥ Craft scissors
- ♥ Acetate, orange
- ♥ Hurricane lamp
- ♥ Votive candle

Instructions:

1. Using a flat brush, paint clay saucer(s) black.

2. Paint rim(s) purple.

3. Paint 1/4" stripes vertically around clay saucer(s) with purple to match rim(s).

4. Using craft scissors, cut a ghost shape from the acetate.

5. Remove backing from acetate and carefully place acetate ghost inside hurricane lamp.

6. Place votive candle in center of clay saucer and place hurricane lamp over the top.

A Witch Flies By

Said the cat to the owl, with a terrible howl, "What is that?"

"Who-o-o!" cried the owl. "I don't know, stupid fowl!" Wailed the cat.

Peek-A-Boo!

Photo on page 10.

Materials & Tools:
- ♥ Craft scissors
- ♥ Acetate, orange

Instructions:

1. Using craft scissors, cut a ghost shape from the acetate.

2. Remove backing from acetate and carefully place acetate ghost inside window.

Spider's Nest

Photo on page 11.

Materials & Tools:

- ✦ Grapevine wreath
- ✦ Black spray paint
- ✦ Polyester spider web
- ✦ Raffia: black, orange, purple
- ✦ Floral wire
- ✦ Hot glue gun and glue sticks
- ✦ Spiders (2)
- ✦ Plastic pumpkins (6)
- ✦ Craft glue
- ✦ Rhinestones, assorted

Instructions:

1. Spray grapevine wreath with black spray paint.

2. Add polyester spider web to wreath as desired.

3. Tie a bow with black, orange, and purple raffia and hot-glue to top, center of wreath.

4. Hot-glue spiders and plastic pumpkins on wreath as desired.

5. Using craft glue, adhere rhinestones to spiders and plastic pumpkins as desired.

Spooks' Night Out

Photo on page 12.

Materials & Tools:

- ♥ Cotton fabric, black, 25½" x 38"
- ♥ Iron and ironing board
- ♥ Fusible web, 2½ yards
- ♥ Cotton fabric, white, 7" x 14"
- ♥ Cotton fabric, gold, 8" square
- ♥ Cotton fabric, orange, ¼ yard
- ♥ Cotton fabric scraps, Halloween-print
- ♥ Cotton fabric strip, Halloween-print, 2" x 19" (2)
- ♥ Fabric scissors
- ♥ Pinking shears
- ♥ Grommets (5)
- ♥ Grommet tool
- ♥ Paintbrushes, flat
- ♥ Wooden dowel, ¼"-diameter x 19½" length
- ♥ Acrylic paint color: black
- ♥ Matte acrylic spray
- ♥ Linen jute

Instructions:

1. Fold black cotton fabric in half to make a 19"-wide x 25½"-high banner. Press on the fold.

2. Using fusible web, adhere top piece of black cotton fabric to bottom piece according to manufacturer's directions.

3. Enlarge Ghost pattern on page 81 to 200%. Using fabric scissors, cut one ghost from white cotton fabric.

4. Enlarge Moon pattern on page 81 to 200%. Using pinking shears, cut one moon from gold cotton fabric.

5. Enlarge Bat patterns on page 81 to 200%. Using fabric scissors, cut two bats from Halloween-print cotton fabric scraps.

6. Reproduce Lettering patterns on page 81 at 100%. Using fabric scissors, cut letters from orange cotton fabric.

7. Adhere Halloween-print cotton fabric strips to black cotton fabric across top and bottom of banner using fusible web.

8. Adhere ghost, moon, and lettering to black cotton fabric as desired using fusible web. Adhere bats to moon.

9. If desired, cut shapes from Halloween-print fabric scraps (such as stars) and adhere as desired.

10. Using a grommet tool, attach grommets, evenly spaced, across top border of banner.

11. Using a flat brush, paint wooden dowel with black.

12. Seal paint with matte acrylic spray.

13. Attach wooden dowel to banner using linen jute threaded through grommets.

14. Tie the ends of string together to form a loop for hanging.

Pumpkin Presents

Photo on page 13.

Materials & Tools for each present:

- ✦ Papier-mâché pumpkin
- ✦ Assorted ribbons, 3 yards
- ✦ Hot glue gun and glue sticks
- ✦ Decorative accessories

Instructions:

1. Place one papier mâché pumpkin in center of each three yard length of ribbon and pull ribbon up each side of pumpkin using grooves in pumpkin as a guide. Twist ribbon at top, wrap ribbon around pumpkin stem, and pull ribbon down each side of pumpkin using grooves as a guide. Repeat until all grooves have been covered.

2. Using the ends of ribbon, which should be close to the same length, tie one bow at top of pumpkin. Then, tie another bow over the first bow.

3. Make a loop from remaining two ribbon ends and, using a hot glue gun and glue sticks, hot-glue in place.

4. Glue decorative accessories to bow or pumpkin as desired.

The 12 Days of Halloween

On the first day of Halloween,
My true love gave to me:
An owl in a dead tree.
Two trick-or-treaters.
Three black cats.
Four skeletons.
Five scary spooks.
Six goblins gobbling.
Seven pumpkins glowing.
Eight monsters shrieking.
Nine ghosts a booing.
Ten ghouls a groaning.
Eleven masks a leering.
Twelve bats a flying.

See-Thru Specter

Photo on page 13.

Materials & Tools:

- ♥ Styrofoam balls, 1" (2), 3½" (1)
- ♥ Styrofoam cone, 8"
- ♥ Hot glue gun and glue sticks
- ♥ Twigs, 4" (2)
- ♥ Cheese cloth, 1 pkg.
- ♥ Fabric scissors
- ♥ Fabric stiffener

Instructions:

1. Using a hot glue gun and glue sticks, hot-glue 3½" Styrofoam ball to top of Styrofoam cone.

2. Push twigs into sides of cone approximately two inches from the top.

3. Hot-glue 1" Styrofoam balls to ends of twigs for hands.

4. Using fabric scissors, cut cheese cloth into a 24" long strip.

5. Using fabric stiffener, prepare cheese cloth according to manufacturer's directions.

6. Place cheese cloth over Styrofoam and twig ghost form. Arrange and position cheese cloth as desired. Allow to dry for several hours.

Costume Party

Photo on page 14.

Materials & Tools:

- ✦ Framed picture (behind glass) of people or animals
- ✦ Sheet of vellum, 17" x 22"
- ✦ Cellophane tape
- ✦ Pencil
- ✦ Craft scissors
- ✦ Re-attachable adhesive
- ✦ Window cleaner

Instructions:

1. Place vellum on glass over framed picture and tape in place.

2. Using a pencil, draw a mask over the face(s) and additional costume ideas, such as tails, wings, etc.

3. Using craft scissors, cut hand-drawn shapes from vellum.

4. Place re-attachable adhesive over backs of vellum shapes and allow to dry thoroughly.

5. Using window cleaner, clean the glass on the framed picture and adhere vellum shapes in position over picture on top of glass. When desired, shapes can easily be removed.

Witch's Brew

Photo on page 15.

Materials & Tools:
+ Fabric, 10" x 18"
+ Fabric, 1" x 5" (2)
+ Fabric, 11" square
+ Pinking shears
+ Craft scissors
+ Craft foam, orange
+ 20 fl. oz. (592 mL) bottle orange soda
+ Hot glue gun and glue sticks
+ Raffia, black
+ Plastic pumpkin
+ Witch hat, black felt
+ Permanent marker, black

Instructions:
1. Using pinking shears, cut 11" square fabric as shown in diagram below.

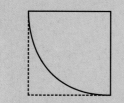

2. Wrap 10" x 18" fabric around bottle of soda for witch's dress. Gather at top. Using a hot glue gun and glue sticks, hot-glue to top of bottle.

3. Fold 1" x 5" fabric strips in half lengthwise and hot-glue along long edge to make arms.

4. Using craft scissors, cut two hands from craft foam and hot-glue in place inside one end of fabric arms. Hot-glue arms in place at witch's sides.

5. Wrap 11" square fabric that has been rounded around bottle for witch's cape. Turn square corners over for cape's collar. Hot-glue in place to secure. Make certain witch's arms show.

6. Tie raffia around neck of bottle and tie in a bow.

7. Hot-glue plastic pumpkin to the fabric on top of bottle and hot-glue witch hat to top of pumpkin.

8. Using a permanent black marker, draw a face on front of pumpkin.

Corny Candles

Photo on page 15.

Materials & Tools for each candle holder:
♥ Clay pot, 2³/₄" diameter
♥ Paintbrushes, flat
♥ Acrylic paint colors: black, orange, purple
♥ Hot glue gun and glue sticks
♥ Tapered candle, 12"
♥ Candy corn

Instructions:
1. Using a flat brush, paint clay pot(s) black.

2. Paint rim(s) orange or purple.

3. Paint 1/4" stripes vertically around clay pot(s) with orange or purple to match rim(s).

4. Using a hot glue gun and glue sticks, hot-glue tapered candle(s) into center, bottom of clay pot(s). Hold in position until secure.

5. Fill clay pot(s) with candy corn.

Candied Apples

Photo on page 15.

Materials & Tools:
+ Carameled apples
+ Candy corn
+ Paring knife

Instructions:
1. Using a paring knife, cut the bottoms off each piece of candy corn.

2. Push remaining piece of candy corn into the caramel as desired.

Why does a mummy keep his bandages in the deep freeze?

He uses them for cold cuts!

Night Delight

Photo on page 16.

Materials & Tools for each pumpkin:

◆ Papier-mâché pumpkin
◆ Paintbrushes, flat
◆ Acrylic paint colors: brown, orange
◆ Pencil
◆ Drill with 1/4" drill bit
◆ Craft knife
◆ Battery-operated light, small

Instructions:

1. Using a flat brush, paint papier-mâché pumpkin with orange.

2. Paint pumpkin stem with brown.

3. Using a pencil, draw desired design(s) onto pumpkin.

4. Using a drill with 1/4" drill bit, carefully drill holes into pumpkin along drawn lines.

5. Using a craft knife, cut a hole in the bottom of pumpkin and add a small battery-operated light inside pumpkin.

Harum Scarum

Photo on page 16.

Materials & Tools for each witch hat:

♥ Witch hat, black felt, 4"
♥ Assorted fabrics
♥ Fabric scissors
♥ Craft glue
♥ Assorted ribbons, cording, or raffia
♥ Decorative accessories
♥ Needle
♥ String

Instructions:

1. Using Circle Streamer pattern on page 88, cut 16 circle streamers from assorted fabrics for each witch hat.

2. Using craft glue, adhere one end of each circle streamer to witch hat around the inside.

3. Using an assortment of ribbons, cording, or raffia, tie a bow around witch hat just above brim.

4. Glue decorative accessories to witch hat as desired.

5. Using a needle and string, make a loop from top of witch hat for hanging. Knots should be placed on the inside point of witch hat.

Scare Mail

Photo on page 17.

Materials & Tools:

◆ Papier-mâché pumpkin, 6" diameter
◆ Craft glue
◆ Craft scissors
◆ Felt, black, 5" x 6"
◆ Witch, 20" tall
◆ Witch hat
◆ Hot glue gun and glue sticks
◆ Wooden doll pin
◆ Wooden bead
◆ Twig, 10"
◆ Small pumpkin
◆ Fabric scissors
◆ Fabric, Halloween print, 2 1/2" wide x 12" long
◆ Artificial spider web
◆ Plastic spiders

Instructions:

1. Using Face pattern on page 94, cut two eyes and one mouth from black felt with craft scissors and glue on papier-mâché pumpkin with craft glue.

2. Using a hot glue gun and glue sticks, hot-glue witch hat on witch.

3. To make witch's broom, hot-glue wooden bead with hole facing upward inside hole in top of wooden doll pin.

4. Hot-glue twig inside hole in wooden bead to secure.

5. Using fabric scissors, cut Halloween-print fabric into strips leaving 1/2" along the top edge uncut.

6. Wrap fabric strip around top of wooden bead, hanging down over wooden doll pin, and hot-glue in place.

7. Hot-glue witch's broom in witch's hand and add artificial spider web and plastic spiders as desired.

8. Hot-glue small pumpkin on top of twig.

Fowl Play

Materials & Tools:

◆ Pine
◆ Transfer paper
◆ Pencil
◆ Jigsaw
◆ Paintbrushes, flat
◆ Liner brush
◆ Gesso
◆ Acrylic paint colors: black, dark blue, fuchsia, rich gold
◆ Matte acrylic spray

Instructions:

1. Before beginning, carefully read General Instructions on pages 4-6.

2. Transfer Fowl Play pattern from page 82 onto pine.

3. Cut crow, including crow's legs, from pine.

4. Seal pine with gesso.

5. Using a flat brush, base-coat crow's body (front and back) with dark blue.

6. Base-coat crow's legs and float-shade around outside edges of crow's body (front and back) with black.

7. Transfer painting details onto one side of crow using Fowl Play pattern on page 82.

8. Using a liner brush, paint crow's beak and bird tracks on crow and crow's legs (front only) with rich gold.

9. Paint eyes on crow (front only) with fuchsia.

10. Paint a comma stroke onto left side of each eye with rich gold.

11. Seal paint with matte acrylic spray.

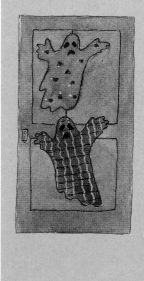

What is a ghost's favorite ride?

The roller ghoster!

26

"Scare" Crow

Materials & Tools:

♥ Pine
♥ Transfer paper
♥ Pencil
♥ Jigsaw
♥ Paintbrushes, flat
♥ Liner brush
♥ Gesso
♥ Acrylic paint colors:
   barn red, black,
   butterscotch, dusty
   purple, forest green,
   metallic champagne
♥ Matte acrylic spray

Instructions:

1. Before beginning, carefully read General Instructions on pages 4-6.

2. Transfer "Scare" Crow pattern from page 82 onto pine.

3. Using a flat brush, base-coat crow's body (front and back) with black.

4. Transfer painting details onto one side of crow using "Scare" Crow pattern on page 82.

5. Float-shade around outside edges of crow's body and add highlights on crow's head and body (front and back) with butterscotch.

6. Using a liner brush, paint a candy corn beak on crow (front only) with butterscotch, barn red, and metallic champagne.

7. Paint eyes on crow (front only) with black.

8. Mix metallic champagne and butterscotch (3:1) to make gold. Paint a comma stroke onto left side of each eye with gold.

9. Mix metallic champagne and dusty purple (3:1) to make purple and mix metallic champagne and forest green (3:1) to make green. Base-coat crow's right leg (front and back) with purple and crow's left leg (front and back) with green.

10. Paint one square patch on crow's body (front only) with purple and one square patch on crow's body (front only) with green. Paint two square patches on crow's left leg (front only) with purple and one square patch on crow's left leg (front only) with green.

11. Paint plaid lines on purple patches with dusty purple and on green patches with forest green.

12. Paint stitches on all patches with gold.

13. Seal paint with matte acrylic spray.

Hare Raising

Materials & Tools:

✦ Pine
✦ Transfer paper
✦ Pencil
✦ Jigsaw
✦ Paintbrushes, flat
✦ Paintbrushes, round
✦ Liner brush
✦ Gesso
✦ Acrylic paint colors:
   black, dark blue,
   fuchsia, purple,
   rich gold, white
✦ Matte acrylic spray

Instructions:

1. Before beginning, carefully read General Instructions on pages 4-6.

2. Transfer Hare Raising pattern from page 82 onto pine.

3. Cut rabbit from pine.

4. Seal pine with gesso.

5. Using a flat brush, base-coat rabbit, except ears and collar, (front and back) with fuchsia.

6. Base-coat rabbit's collar (front and back) with purple.

7. Transfer painting details onto both sides of rabbit using Hare Raising pattern on page 82.

8. Using a round brush, paint diamonds on rabbit's ears (front and back). On the left ear, paint half the diamonds with rich gold and remaining diamonds with purple. On the right ear, paint half the diamonds with white and remaining diamonds with dark blue.

9. Float-shade around outside edges of rabbit's head, body, and legs (front and back) with black.

10. Float-highlight around outside edges of rabbit's collar (front and back) with white.

11. Using a round brush, paint diamonds on rabbit's body with gesso. Then, paint top diamond with dark blue and middle diamond with white. On the set of three diamonds, paint top diamond with dark blue, middle diamond with rich gold, and bottom diamond with purple.

12. Using a liner brush, paint eyes and a nose on rabbit (front only) with black.

13. Add a dot on each ruffle on rabbit's collar (front and back) with rich gold.

14. Seal paint with matte acrylic spray.

28

Scaredy Cat

Materials & Tools:

♥ Pine
♥ Transfer paper
♥ Pencil
♥ Jigsaw
♥ Paintbrushes, flat
♥ Liner brush
♥ Gesso
♥ Acrylic paint colors: black, dusty purple, metallic champagne
♥ Matte acrylic spray

Instructions:

1. Before beginning, carefully read General Instructions on pages 4-6.

2. Transfer Scaredy Cat pattern from page 83 onto pine.

3. Cut cat from pine.

4. Seal pine with gesso.

5. Mix metallic champagne and dusty purple (3:1) to make purple. Using a flat brush, base-coat cat (front and back) with purple.

6. Transfer painting details onto one side of cat using Scaredy Cat pattern on page 83.

7. Float-shade around outside edges of cat's head, body, and legs (front and back), around outer edge of cat's tail (front and back), and inside each of cat's legs with black.

8. To make stripes, float-shade around all previously float-shaded areas, moving flat brush from side-to-side, with black.

9. Float-shade inside cat's ears (front only) with metallic champagne.

10. Using a liner brush, paint eyes and a nose on cat (front only) with black. Add dots around cat's nose with black. Paint short lines on cat's feet to make claws with black.

11. Wash around all outside edges (front and back) with black.

12. Seal paint with matte acrylic spray.

Jack-O-Magic

Materials & Tools:

✦ Pine
✦ Transfer paper
✦ Pencil
✦ Jigsaw
✦ Paintbrushes, flat
✦ Liner brush
✦ Gesso
✦ Acrylic paint colors: antique copper, black, dark blue, dark teal, fuchsia, metallic gold, rich gold
✦ Matte acrylic spray

Instructions:

1. Before beginning, carefully read General Instructions on pages 4-6.

2. Transfer Jack-O-Magic pattern from page 83 onto pine.

3. Cut pumpkins from pine.

4. Seal pine with gesso.

5. Using a flat brush, base-coat pumpkins (front and back) with rich gold.

6. Paint bottom part of hat (front and back) with dark teal.

7. Paint top part of hat (front and back) with fuchsia.

8. Paint tiny pumpkins on each hat point (front and back) with rich gold.

9. Transfer painting details onto both sides of pumpkins using Jack-O-Magic pattern on page 83.

10. Float-shade indentations on pumpkins (front and back) with antique copper.

11. Float-shade around top edges of crown points on hat (front and back) with dark blue.

12. Wash over fuchsia on top part of hat (front and back) with metallic gold.

13. Using a liner brush, outline crown with metallic gold. Add two metallic gold dots in each section (front and back).

14. Paint diamonds on crown (front and back) with fuchsia.

15. Paint faces on tiny pumpkins on hat points (front only) with black.

16. Paint a face on top pumpkin (front only) with black.

17. Paint swirls and stars on bottom pumpkin (front only) with metallic gold.

18. Seal paint with matte acrylic spray.

Country Bumpkin Pumpkin

Materials & Tools:

♥ Pine
♥ Transfer paper
♥ Pencil
♥ Jigsaw
♥ Paintbrushes, flat
♥ Liner brush
♥ Gesso
♥ Acrylic paint colors: barn red, black, butterscotch, metallic champagne, rich brown
♥ Matte acrylic spray

Instructions:

1. Before beginning, carefully read General Instructions on pages 4-6.

2. Transfer Country Bumpkin Pumpkin pattern from page 83 onto pine.

3. Cut pumpkins from pine.

4. Seal pine with gesso.

5. Mix metallic champagne and butterscotch (3:1) to make gold. Using a flat brush, base-coat pumpkins (front and back) with gold.

6. Paint hat (front and back) with barn red.

7. Transfer painting details onto both sides of pumpkins using Country Bumpkin Pumpkin pattern on page 83.

8. Float-shade indentations on pumpkins (front and back) with black.

9. Using a liner brush, paint eyes and a mouth on top pumpkin (front only) with black.

10. Paint a candy corn nose on top pumpkin (front only), three on middle pumpkin (front only) to make buttons, and three on bottom pumpkin (front only) with butterscotch, barn red, and metallic champagne.

11. Paint vertical lines on hat (front and back) with metallic champagne, then paint vertical lines next to metallic champagne-colored lines with rich brown.

12. Paint double horizontal lines on hat (front and back) with black.

13. Float-shade around outer edge of hat (front and back) with black.

14. Seal paint with matte acrylic spray.

Spell Bloomed

Materials & Tools:

◆ Pine
◆ Transfer paper
◆ Pencil
◆ Jigsaw
◆ Paintbrushes, flat
◆ Paintbrushes, round
◆ Liner brush
◆ Gesso
◆ Acrylic paint colors: antique copper, black, dark teal, fuchsia, metallic gold, purple, rich gold
◆ Matte acrylic spray

Instructions:

1. Before beginning, carefully read General Instructions on pages 4-6.

2. Transfer Spell Bloomed pattern from page 84 onto pine.

3. Cut sunflowers from pine.

4. Seal pine with gesso.

5. Transfer painting details onto both sides of sunflowers using Spell Bloomed pattern on page 84.

6. Using a flat brush, base-coat sunflowers' centers (front and back) with rich gold.

7. Base-coat sunflowers' stems and leaves (front and back) with dark teal.

8. Base-coat three sunflower petals on each sunflower (front and back) with fuchsia.

9. Using a round brush, paint diamonds on re-maining four sunflower petals on each sunflower (front and back) alternately with dark teal and purple.

10. Float-shade indentations on pumpkins (front and back) and paint pumpkin stems on sunflowers' centers (front only) with antique copper.

11. Float-shade around sunflowers' stems and leaves (front and back) with metallic gold.

12. Using a liner brush, paint faces on sunflowers' centers (front only) and line around pumpkin stems with black.

13. Randomly paint dots and stars on fuchsia-colored sunflower petals and line each diamond on remaining sunflower petals with metallic gold.

14. Dry-brush sunflowers' stems and leaves with metallic gold.

15. Seal paint with matte acrylic spray.

Tongue Twisters

Try saying these tongue twisters three times really fast!

• A slice of spicy pumpkin pie.
• Groovy ghoulish ghosts.
• Creepy critters come crawling.

Candy Cornflower

Materials & Tools:

- ♥ Pine
- ♥ Transfer paper
- ♥ Pencil
- ♥ Jigsaw
- ♥ Paintbrushes, flat
- ♥ Liner brush
- ♥ Gesso
- ♥ Acrylic paint colors: barn red, black, butterscotch, forest green, metallic champagne, rich brown
- ♥ Matte acrylic spray

Instructions:

1. Before beginning, carefully read General Instructions on pages 4-6.

2. Transfer Candy Cornflower pattern from page 85 onto pine.

3. Cut sunflowers from pine.

4. Seal pine with gesso.

5. Transfer painting details onto both sides of sunflowers using Candy Cornflower pattern on page 85.

6. Mix metallic champagne and butterscotch (3:1) to make gold. Using a flat brush, base-coat sunflowers' centers (front and back) and three sunflower petals on each sunflower (front and back) with gold.

7. Mix metallic champagne and forest green (3:1) to make green. Base-coat sunflowers' stems and leaves (front and back) with green.

8. Base-coat remaining four sunflower petals on each sunflower (front and back) with barn red.

9. Float-shade indentations on pumpkins (front and back) with black.

10. Paint pumpkin stems on sunflowers'

centers (front only) with rich brown.

11. Float-shade around sunflowers' stems and leaves (front and back) with metallic champagne.

12. Using a liner brush, paint eyes and a mouth on sunflowers' centers (front only) and line around pumpkin stems with black.

13. Paint a candy corn nose on pumpkins (front only) and two on each gold-colored sunflower petal (front and back) with butterscotch, barn red, and metallic champagne.

14. Paint vertical lines on each barn red-colored sunflower petal (front and back) with metallic champagne, then paint vertical lines next to metallic champagne-colored lines with rich brown.

15. Paint double horizontal lines on barn red-colored sunflower petals (front and back) with black.

16. Dry-brush sunflowers' stems and leaves with butterscotch.

17. Seal paint with matte acrylic spray.

How To Convert Color Schemes From "Magical" To "Country"

The projects from pages 35-78 have been designed to offer two color scheme choices.

The first set of materials and tools lists and instructions are for projects using a "magical" color scheme. Immediately following each project is a set of materials and tools lists and instructions to aid in converting the projects to a country color scheme.

Sample Project

Materials & Tools:

✦ Pine
✦ Primer/sealer
✦ Drill with drill bit
✦ Acrylic paint colors: emerald green
✦ Sparkle glaze
✦ Pumpkin-shaped bells, 2" (2)
✦ Eye screws, ¹/₂" (2)
✦ Jump rings, 6mm (2)

Instructions:

1. Cut pine into sample shape.
2. Seal shape with primer/sealer.
3. Drill one hole in each side of sample shape.
4. Using a flat brush, base-coat sample shape with emerald green.
5. Paint over sample shape with sparkle glaze.

6. Attach one pumpkin-shaped bell to each side of sample shape using eye screws and jump rings.

When making projects in the magical color scheme, follow the materials and tools lists and instructions exactly, regardless of the color of ✦✦ shown.

... using a country color scream

Materials & Tools:

♥ Acrylic paint color: country gold
♥ Pumpkin-shaped bell, 2"
♥ Eye screw, ¹/₂"
♥ Jump ring, 6mm

Instructions:

3. Drill one hole in top of sample shape.

4. Using a flat brush, base-coat sample shape with country gold.

6. Attach pumpkin-shaped bell to top of sample shape using eye screw and jump ring.

When making projects in the country color scheme, follow the materials and tools lists, changing those marked with an orange ✦ and replacing that item with the replacement item listed in the materials and tools lists marked with an orange ♥. In some cases, the change is only in the quantity of that particular item that is needed.

When no replacement item is listed, that item is not used for the country-colored project. When a new item appears, that item was not used for the magical-colored project.

When making projects in the country color scheme, follow instructions for magical-colored projects, substituting the new numerical steps.

In this example, steps one, two, and five would be exactly the same as the magical-colored project. Steps three, four, and six were altered in some way.

Artwork

The additional pieces of artwork featured throughout this publication have been provided to offer additional Halloween decorating tips and ideas!

Brewing Halloween Magic

Stacked Jack

Photo on page 36.

Materials & Tools:

- ◆ Pine, 4' x 6' x ½"
- ◆ Primer/sealer
- ◆ Branches (2)
- ◆ Drill with drill bit
- ◆ Acrylic paint colors: emerald green, purple
- ◆ Sparkle glaze
- ◆ Pumpkin-shaped bells, 2" (4)
- ◆ Eye screws, ½" (4)
- ◆ Jump rings, 6mm (4)
- ◆ Awl
- ◆ Craft glue
- ◆ Rhinestones, round, assorted sizes and colors
- ◆ Scarf, optional
- ◆ See additional list of materials and tools needed for Jack-O-Magic on page 30.

Instructions:

1. Enlarge Stacked Jack #1 pattern on page 86 to 500%.

2. Follow instructions on page 30 to make a Jack-O-Magic, using primer/sealer to seal pine.

3. Cut a base from pine and cut notches in body and base using Stacked Jack #1 pattern on page 86.

4. Drill one hole in each side of middle pumpkin to accommodate branches.

5. Seal pine base, branches, and bells with primer/sealer.

6. Using a flat brush, base-coat base (both sides) and bells with rich gold.

7. Paint leaves with emerald green.

8. Paint branches with black, then add touches of fuchsia, dark teal, and purple.

9. Coat branches with sparkle glaze.

10. Join body and base.

11. Using an awl, make a hole in each hat point and screw one eye screw into each hole.

12. Using jump rings, attach bells to eye screws.

13. Place branches into drilled holes in sides of body to make arms.

14. Seal paint with matte acrylic spray.

15. Glue a rhinestone in the center of each swirl and star and over each dot at ends of stars on bottom pumpkin.

16. Glue rhinestones on hat over metallic gold dots and fuchsia diamonds.

17. If desired, tie a scarf around neck.

... using a country color scream

Photo on page 71.

Materials & Tools:

- ♥ Acrylic paint colors: forest green
- ♥ Pumpkin-shaped bell, 2"
- ♥ Eye screw, ½"
- ♥ Jump ring, 6mm
- ♥ See additional list of materials and tools needed for Country Bumpkin Pumpkin on page 31.

Instructions:

1. Enlarge Stacked Jack #2 pattern on page 86 to 570%.

2. Follow instructions on page 31 to make a Country Bumpkin Pumpkin, using primer/ sealer to seal pine.

3. Cut a base from pine and cut notches in body and base using Stacked Jack #2 pattern on page 86.

6. Using a flat brush, base-coat base (both sides) and bell with gold.

7. Mix metallic champagne and forest green (3:1) to make green. Paint leaves with green.

11. Using an awl, make a hole in hat point and screw eye screw into hole.

12. Using a jump ring, attach bell to eye screw.

13. Place unpainted branches into drilled holes in sides of body to make arms.

Foaming At The Fount

Photo on page 37.

Materials & Tools:

✦ Fountain, 26" high
✦ Primer/sealer
✦ String of lights, optional
✦ Electrical tape, optional
✦ Dry ice, optional
✦ Water, optional
✦ Hot glue gun and glue sticks
✦ See additional lists of materials and tools needed for Crows' Feet crows on this page and for Hare Raising rabbit on page 28.

Instructions:

1. Enlarge Fowl Play pattern (without legs) on page 82 to 185% and to 250%.

2. Enlarge Hare Raising pattern on page 82 to 300%.

3. Follow instructions on this page to make two Crows' Feet crows, using primer/sealer to seal pine. <u>Do not allow pine for crows' legs, as crows' legs should not be cut out.</u>

4. Follow instructions on page 28 to make a Hare Raising rabbit, using primer/sealer to seal pine.

5. If desired, add a string of lights around fountain, using electrical tape to secure.

6. If desired, add dry ice and water to fountain.

7. Stand rabbit next to fountain and set both crows on edge of fountain. Hot-glue in place.

Crows' Feet

Photo on page 38.

Materials & Tools for 2 Crows:

✦ Pine, 2' x 4' x ½"
✦ Drill with drill bit
✦ Primer/sealer
✦ Braided wire
✦ Wire cutters
✦ See additional lists of materials and tools needed for Fowl Play crow on page 26.

Instructions:

1. Enlarge Fowl Play pattern on page 82 to 160%.

2. Follow instructions on page 26 to make two Fowl Play crows, using primer/sealer to seal pine.

3. Drill two holes through bottom of front side of each crow to accommodate braided wire.

4. Using wire cutters, cut braided wire into 18" lengths.

5. For each crow's legs and feet, begin at 9" and bend braided wire at an angle, then bend it back 1" to make crow's first toe. Repeat process allowing 1½" to make crow's second toe. Repeat process allowing 1" to make crow's third toe. Bend braided wire back and twist it around the 9" piece of braided wire to make crow's back toe. See diagram below.

6. Push top of each 9" piece of braided wire through drilled holes in bottom of each crow and wrap it in a circular motion to secure.

... using a country color scream

Photo on page 71.

Instructions:

1. Use the "Scare" Crow pattern on page 82 and paint according to color designations given on page 27.

... using a country color scream

Photo on page 72.

Instructions:

1. Use the "Scare" Crow pattern on page 82 and paint according to color designations given on page 27.

All Tied Up!

Photo on pages 56-57.

Materials & Tools:

✦ Grapevine and leaf garland, 6'
✦ Mesh ribbon (wired), metallic gold, 2½"-wide (3 yards)
✦ Craft scissors

Instructions:

1. Cut mesh ribbon into lengths varying from 10" to 15".

2. Randomly attach each length of mesh ribbon to garland by twisting one end of mesh ribbon around grapevine stems.

3. Twist mesh ribbon ends into spirals.

Harvest Garland

Photo on page 71.

Materials & Tools:

♥ Bleached bell cups (6)
♥ Pliers
♥ Paintbrushes, flat
♥ Liner brush
♥ Acrylic paint colors: barn red, black, butterscotch, metallic champagne
♥ Wood excelsior
♥ Triangle-shaped cut outs, 3½" high x ¼" wide (3)
♥ Matte acrylic spray
♥ Raffia
♥ Floral wire
♥ Ribbon (wired), light green, 1½"-wide (3 yards)
♥ Craft scissors
♥ Hot glue gun and glue sticks
♥ Dried myrtle leaves, autumn colors

Instructions:

1. Using pliers, remove stems from bell cups to make pumpkins.

2. Mix metallic champagne and butterscotch (3:1) to make gold. Float-shade indentations on pumpkins with gold.

3. Using a liner brush, paint eyes and a mouth on each pumpkin with black.

4. Paint a candy corn nose on each pumpkin with butterscotch, barn red, and metallic champagne.

5. Fill each pumpkin with wood excelsior.

6. Paint each triangle-shaped cut out (front and back) with butterscotch, barn red, and metallic champagne to resemble candy corn.

7. Seal paint on pumpkins and candy corn with matte acrylic spray.

8. On a flat surface, straighten raffia and pull it to extend its length to eight feet.

9. Find center of raffia and, using floral wire, wire tightly, twisting ends of wire together and tucking into raffia.

10. Measure two feet from center of raffia in each direction and repeat process for wiring.

11. Place ribbon along top of raffia garland and, leaving a two foot tail on each end, twist ribbon and tie into place around each wired section. Trim ends as desired.

12. Hot-glue two pumpkins and one candy corn at each wired section. Hot-glue myrtle leaves around each cluster as desired.

Trick-or-Tweet

Photo on page 38.

Materials & Tools:

- Papier-mâché pumpkin, 8½" diameter x 6" high
- Craft knife
- Terra cotta pot spray sealer
- Air-drying clay, 3-4 oz. bag
- Toothpick
- Transfer paper
- Pencil
- Paintbrushes, flat
- Stipple brush
- Fine-point permanent marker, black
- Acrylic paint colors: antique copper, black, dark teal, fuchsia, purple, rich gold, white

- Silk leaves, 1" (6); 2" (13-15); 3½" (9-11)
- Small twig, 1"

- Wooden dowel, 1" diameter x 36" length
- Plastic cauldron, black, 11" diameter x 8½" high
- Adhesive spray
- Hot glue gun and glue sticks
- Matte acrylic spray
- Industrial-strength glue
- Plaster of paris, 5 lbs.
- Florist's foam
- Metallic bronze floral hair
- Craft glue
- Rhinestones, assorted shapes, sizes, and colors

Instructions:

1. Before beginning, carefully read General Instructions on pages 4-6.

2. Using a craft knife, cut a 1¼" circular hole in front of papier-mâché pumpkin, approximately 1½" from bottom, to make birdhouse opening. Cut a 1" circular hole, centered on bottom of pumpkin, to accommodate wooden dowel to make birdhouse stand.

3. Seal papier-mâché pumpkin (inside and out) with terra cotta pot spray sealer.

4. Sculpt a pumpkin stem around existing papier-mâché pumpkin stem with air-drying clay and make indentations in stem with a toothpick.

5. Using a flat brush, base-coat papier-mâché pumpkin with rich gold.

6. Float-shade indentations on pumpkin with antique copper.

7. Using Birdhouse Window pattern below, make three patterns: one large, one medium, and one small. Transfer one large, one medium, and three small windows onto front of pumpkin as desired.

Birdhouse Window

8. Paint windows, including window moulding and cross members, with white.

9. Float-shade around window moulding and cross members with rich gold.

10. Add dots in windows and base-coat sculpted clay pumpkin stem with antique copper.

11. Using the 1" silk leaves, paint four with fuchsia and two with rich gold. Using the 2" and the 3½" silk leaves, paint approximately six each with the following colors: antique copper, fuchsia, rich gold, and dark teal.

12. Stipple over all fuchsia-colored silk leaves with antique copper and over all rich gold-colored silk leaves with fuchsia.

13. Base-coat small twig with antique copper.

14. Base-coat wooden dowel with fuchsia.

15. Spray cauldron with adhesive spray and allow to dry thoroughly. This must be done so the acrylic paint will adhere to the plastic.

16. Base-coat cauldron with purple.

17. Randomly transfer swirls and stars around windows on front of pumpkin and around cauldron using Swirls and Stars patterns on page 94.

18. Using a liner brush, paint swirls and stars on pumpkin and on cauldron with antique copper.

19. Hot-glue the 1" silk leaves to front of pumpkin just above birdhouse opening and the remaining silk leaves around pumpkin stem on top of pumpkin. Hot-glue small twig to front of pumpkin just below birdhouse opening to make a bird's perch.

20. Once again, seal papier-mâché pumpkin (inside and out), including all embellishments, with terra cotta pot spray sealer.

21. Seal paint with matte acrylic spray.

22. Using a black fine-point permanent marker, add lined details around windows.

23. Apply industrial-strength glue around edges of circular hole in bottom of papier-mâché pumpkin. Insert wooden dowel into hole. Lay pumpkin and

wooden dowel on a flat surface and prop up wooden dowel so bottom of pumpkin is at a 90° angle.

24. Mix plaster of paris according to manufacturer's directions and fill cauldron $\frac{1}{2}$ to $\frac{3}{4}$ full. Place wooden dowel into plaster of paris in center of cauldron and prop up so birdhouse is level.

25. Glue florist's foam inside cauldron around wooden dowel. Top with metallic bronze floral hair and hot-glue in place.

26. Glue rhinestones around windows on front of pumpkin and randomly on a few silk leaves. Use photograph on page 38 for rhinestone placement.

27. If desired, make Stakes From The Heart and poke them into florist's foam inside cauldron. See instructions on how to make Stakes From The Heart on page 46.

28. If desired, make one or more Crows' Feet crows and hot-glue them on front edge of cauldron. See instructions on how to make Crows' Feet crows on page 42.

... using a country color scream

Photo on page 72.

Materials & Tools:

♥ Acrylic paint colors: barn red, butterscotch, forest green, metallic champagne, rich brown
♥ Spanish moss

Instructions:

5. Mix metallic champagne and butterscotch (3:1) to make gold. Using a flat brush, base-coat papier-mâché pumpkin with gold.

6. Float-shade indentations on pumpkin with rich brown.

7. Using Birdhouse Window pattern below, make three patterns: one large, one medium, and one small. Transfer one large, one medium, and three small windows onto front of pumpkin as desired.

Birdhouse Window

8. Mix metallic champagne and forest green (3:1) to make green. Paint windows with green adding window moulding and cross members with metallic champagne.

9. Float-shade around window moulding and cross members with butterscotch. Paint three candy corn around each window with butterscotch, barn red, and metallic champagne.

10. Add dots in windows and base-coat sculpted clay pumpkin stem with rich brown.

11. Using the 1" silk leaves, paint two with rich brown, two with gold, and two with green. Using the 2" and the 3½" silk leaves, paint approximately six each with the following colors: gold and green. Paint approximately twelve with rich brown.

12. Stipple over all gold-colored silk leaves with butterscotch, over all green-colored silk leaves with rich brown, and over all rich brown-colored leaves with barn red.

13. Base-coat small twig with rich brown.

14. Base-coat wooden dowel with green.

16. Base-coat cauldron with rich brown.

17. Randomly transfer candy corn around cauldron using Candy Corn pattern on page 94.

18. Using a liner brush, paint candy corn on cauldron with butter-scotch, barn red, and metallic champagne.

25. Glue florist's foam inside cauldron around wooden dowel. Top with Spanish moss and hot-glue in place.

27. If desired, make Stakes From The Heart and poke them into florist's foam inside cauldron. See instructions on how to make Stakes From The Heart on page 46.

28. If desired, make one or more Crows' Feet crows and hot-glue them inside cauldron or on top of birdhouse. See instructions on how to make Crows' Feet crows on page 42.

Stakes From The Heart

Photo on page 38.

Materials & Tools for 3 Stakes:

✦ Pine, 2' x 4' x ¹⁄₂"
✦ Wooden dowels, ¹⁄₄" diameter x 14" length (3)
✦ Drill with drill bits
✦ Primer/sealer
✦ Wire, 26-gauge
✦ Wire cutters
✦ Wood glue
✦ See additional lists of materials and tools needed for Spell Bloomed sunflower on page 32.

Instructions:

1. Enlarge Stakes From The Heart patterns on page 88 to 135%.

2. Follow instructions on page 32 to make a Spell Bloomed sunflower, using primer/sealer to seal pine. Plant stakes differ from Spell Bloomed sunflowers only because plant stake sunflower centers and leaves are cut separately and wooden dowels replace sun-flower stems. All paint colors and techniques remain the same.

3. Drill one hole in the bottom of each sun-flower petal piece to accommodate wooden dowels.

4. Drill one hole through each sunflower leaf and through wooden dowels at 2¹⁄₂" intervals to accommodate 26-gauge wire.

5. Glue sunflower centers onto sunflower petals.

6. Glue wooden dowels into drilled holes in bottom of sunflower petals to make sun-flower stems.

7. Using wire cutters, cut 26-gauge wire into 4" lengths.

8. For each sunflower leaf, push one 4" wire through hole in leaf and through hole in wooden dowel. Bring both ends up and tightly twist ends together. Spiral each loose end of wire.

9. Repeat process until all sunflower leaves are attached to sunflower stems.

... using a country color scream

Photo on page 72.

Materials & Tools for 3 Stakes:

♥ See additional lists of materials and tools needed for Candy Cornflower on page 33.

Instructions:

2. Follow instructions on page 33 to make a Candy Cornflower, using primer/sealer to seal pine. Plant stakes differ from Candy Cornflowers only be-cause plant stake sunflower centers and leaves are cut separately and wooden dowels replace sunflower stems. All paint colors and techniques remain the same.

Hang Man

Photo on page 39.

Materials & Tools:

- ✦ Strata core, 20" x 30"
- ✦ Craft knife
- ✦ Adhesive spray
- ✦ Branches (2)
- ✦ Acrylic paint color: purple
- ✦ Sparkle glaze
- ✦ Awl
- ✦ Mesh ribbon (wired), fuchsia, 1/2"-wide (5 1/2 yards) or Raffia
- ✦ Craft scissors
- ✦ Craft glue
- ✦ Rhinestones, round, assorted sizes and colors
- ✦ See additional list of materials and tools needed for Jack-O-Magic on page 30.

Instructions:

1. Enlarge Hang Man #1 pattern on page 87 to 400%.

2. Follow instructions on page 30 to make a Jack-O-Magic, using a craft knife to cut pieces from strata core instead of pine, and spraying all pieces with adhesive spray before sealing with gesso.

3. Seal branches with gesso.

4. Paint branches with black, then add touches of fuchsia, dark teal, and purple.

5. Coat branches with sparkle glaze.

6. Using an awl, make one hole in top of hat and two holes in bottom of hat. Make two holes each in tops of top, middle, and bottom pumpkins and make two holes each in bottoms of top and middle pumpkins.

7. Cut fuchsia mesh ribbon or raffia into 12" lengths.

8. Attach one length of mesh ribbon or raffia through hole in top of hat and tie a knot for hanging.

9. Join hat to top pumpkin, top pumpkin to middle pumpkin, and middle pumpkin to bottom pumpkin by attaching lengths of mesh ribbon through holes and allowing 1 1/2" of space between hat and top pumpkin and between each pumpkin. Tie into knots to secure mesh ribbon or raffia.

10. Twist mesh ribbon ends into spirals.

11. Push branches into sides of middle pumpkin to make arms and glue in place.

12. Glue a rhinestone in the center of each swirl and star and over each dot at ends of stars on bottom pumpkin.

13. Glue rhinestones on hat over metallic gold dots and fuchsia diamonds.

... using a country color scream

Photo on page 71.

Materials & Tools:

- ♥ Raffia
- ♥ Hot curling iron
- ♥ See additional list of materials and tools needed for Country Bumpkin Pumpkin on page 31.

Instructions:

1. Enlarge Hang Man #2 pattern on page 87 to 425%.

2. Follow instructions on page 31 to make a Country Bumpkin Pumpkin, using a craft knife to cut pieces from strata core instead of pine, and spraying all pieces with adhesive spray before sealing with gesso.

10. Using a hot curling iron, curl raffia ends.

11. Push unpainted branches into sides of middle pumpkin to make arms and glue in place.

What kind of pants do ghosts wear?

BOO jeans!

Perennial Pretender

Photo on page 40.

Materials & Tools:

- Wooden fence
- Transfer paper
- Pencil
- Paintbrushes, flat
- Paintbrushes, round
- Primer/sealer
- Acrylic paint colors: fuchsia, metallic gold, purple
- Craft glue
- Rhinestones, assorted shapes, sizes, and colors
- Matte acrylic spray
- String of lights, optional

Instructions:

1. Before beginning, carefully read General Instructions on pages 4-6.

2. Seal wooden fence with primer/sealer.

3. Using a flat brush, base-coat wooden fence with fuchsia. Wash over fuchsia with purple.

4. Randomly transfer swirls and stars onto one side of wooden fence using Swirls and Stars patterns on page 94.

5. Using a round brush, paint swirls and stars on fence with metallic gold.

6. Seal paint with matte acrylic spray.

7. Glue a rhinestone in the center of each swirl and star on wooden fence.

8. If desired, add a string of lights to wooden fence.

... using a country color scream

Photo on page 71.

Materials & Tools:

- Acrylic paint colors: barn red, butterscotch, dusty purple, metallic champagne

Instructions:

3. Mix metallic champagne and dusty purple (3:1) to make purple. Using a flat brush, base-coat wooden fence with purple.

4. Randomly transfer candy corn onto one side of wooden fence using Candy Corn patterns on page 94.

5. Using a round brush, paint candy corn on fence with butterscotch, barn red, and metallic champagne.

How do baby ghosts keep their feet warm?

They wear BOO-tees!

Spook Weed

Photo on page 40.

Materials & Tools:

✦ Galvanized metal, 3' x 3'
✦ Stretcher bar, 1/2" x 26"
✦ Transfer paper
✦ Pencil
✦ Tin snips
✦ Clamps
✦ Drill with drill bit
✦ Screws (3)
✦ Nuts (3)
✦ Medium-grit sandpaper
✦ Pencil
✦ Paintbrushes, flat
✦ Paintbrushes, round
✦ Liner brush
✦ Primer/sealer
✦ Acrylic paint colors: antique copper, black, dark teal, emerald green, fuchsia, metallic gold, purple, rich gold
✦ Industrial-strength glue
✦ Matte acrylic spray

Instructions:

1. Before beginning, carefully read General Instructions on pages 4-6.

2. Transfer Spook Weed patterns from page 89 onto galvanized metal.

3. Using tin snips, cut sunflower from metal.

4. Slightly bend petals for center sunflower petals.

5. Very carefully sand all cut edges of metal so they are not sharp.

6. Lay back petals on top of stretcher bar. Center petals on top of back petals, positioning center petals between back petals. Clamp together and drill a hole to accommodate screw through the center.

7. Push a screw through the drilled hole and fasten with a nut.

8. Lay stem with leaves on top of stretcher bar 2" from bottom of back petals. Clamp together and drill one hole through the top and one through the bottom to accommodate screws.

9. Push a screw through the drilled holes and fasten with nuts.

10. Seal metal with primer/sealer.

11. Using a pencil, lightly draw diamonds on center petals. Using a round brush, paint diamonds alternately with dark teal and purple.

12. Using a flat brush, base-coat back petals with fuchsia.

13. Randomly transfer swirls and stars onto back petals using Swirls and Stars patterns on page 94.

14. Using a liner brush, paint swirls and stars on back petals with metallic gold.

15. Outline dark teal- and purple-colored diamonds with metallic gold.

16. Base-coat stem and leaves with dark teal.

17. While paint is wet, add emerald green to center of stem and leaves, blending into dark teal.

18. Base-coat sunflower's center with rich gold.

19. Dry-brush leaves with metallic gold.

20. Float-shade indentations on pumpkin with antique copper.

21. Using a liner brush, paint a face on pumpkin with black.

22. Paint a stem on pumpkin with antique copper.

23. Glue sunflower's center in middle of center petals.

24. Seal paint with matte acrylic spray.

Outside Decorating Tips

• Play a recording of scary sounds.

• Hang a string of lights with black and orange bulbs.

• Place artificial spider web in trees and bushes.

• Place dry ice in any fountain or bird bath with a little water to create fog.

... using a country color scream

Photo on page 71.

Materials & Tools:

♥ Acrylic paint colors: barn red, black, butterscotch, forest green, metallic champagne, rich brown

Instructions:

11. Using a flat brush, base-coat center petals with barn red.

12. Mix metallic champagne and butterscotch (3:1) to make gold. Base-coat back petals with gold. Paint vertical lines on each barn red-colored sunflower petal with metallic champagne, then paint vertical lines next to metallic champagne-colored lines with rich brown. Paint double horizontal lines on barn red-colored sunflower petals with black.

13. Randomly transfer candy corn onto back petals using Candy Corn pattern on page 94.

14. Using a liner brush, paint candy corn on back petals with butterscotch, barn red, and metallic champagne.

16. Mix metallic champagne and forest green (3:1) to make green. Base-coat stem and leaves with green.

17. Float-shade around stem and leaves with black.

18. Base-coat sunflower's center and dry-brush petals with gold.

20. Float-shade indentations on pumpkin with black.

21. Using a liner brush, paint eyes and a mouth on pumpkin with black. Paint a candy corn nose on pumpkin with butterscotch, barn red, and metallic champagne.

22. Paint a stem on pumpkin with rich brown.

It's A Scream!

Photo on page 50.

Materials & Tools:

- ✦ Pine, 4' x 8' x ½"
- ✦ Sparkle glaze
- ✦ Industrial-strength glue
- ✦ Clamps
- ✦ Hinge assemblies (6)
- ✦ Screwdriver
- ✦ See additional lists of materials and tools needed for Fowl Play crow on page 26, Hare Raising rabbit on page 28, Jack-O-Magic on page 30, and Spell Bloomed sunflower on page 32.

Instructions:

1. Enlarge Screen Fence pattern on page 90 to 475%.
2. Enlarge Fowl Play pattern on page 82 to 335%.
3. Enlarge Hare Raising pattern on page 82 to 400%.
4. Enlarge Jack-O-Magic pattern on page 83 to 400%.
5. Enlarge Spell Bloomed pattern on page 84 to 400%.
6. Cut four screen fences from pine.
7. Seal pine screen fences with gesso.
8. Using a flat brush, base-coat screen fences (front and back) with black.
9. Float-shade vertical lines on screen fences with fuchsia.
10. Coat screen fences with sparkle glaze.
11. Follow instructions on page 26 to make a Fowl Play crow.
12. Follow instructions on page 28 to make a Hare Raising rabbit.
13. Follow instructions on page 30 to make a Jack-O-Magic.
14. Follow instructions on page 32 to make a Spell Bloomed sunflower.
15. Glue each character to one piece of screen fence, aligning bottoms.
16. Clamp characters in position until glue has thoroughly dried.
17. Attach screen fences together using hinge assemblies.

... using a country color scream

Photo on page 76.

Materials & Tools:

- ♥ Pumpkin-shaped bell, 2"
- ♥ Eye screw, ½"
- ♥ Jump ring, 6mm
- ♥ Awl
- ♥ See additional lists of materials and tools needed for "Scare" Crow on page 27, Scaredy Cat on page 29, Country Bumpkin Pumpkin on page 31, and Candy Cornflower on page 33.

Instructions:

2. Enlarge "Scare" Crow pattern on page 82 to 335%.
3. Enlarge Scaredy Cat pattern on page 83 to 400%.
4. Enlarge Country Bumpkin Pumpkin pattern on page 83 to 400%.
5. Enlarge Candy Cornflower pattern on page 85 to 400%.
6. Cut four screen fences from pine.
7. Seal pine screen fences and bell with gesso.
8. Using a flat brush, base-coat screen fences (front and back) with barn red.

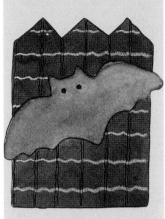

9. Float-shade vertical lines on screen fences with black.
10. Base-coat bell with gold.
11. Follow instructions on page 27 to make a "Scare" Crow.
12. Follow instructions on page 29 to make a Scaredy Cat.
13. Follow instructions on page 31 to make a Country Bumpkin Pumpkin.
14. Follow instructions on page 33 to make a Candy Cornflower.
18. Using an awl, make a hole in hat point and screw eye screw into hole.
19. Using a jump ring, attach bell to eye screw.

Hanging Trees

Photo on pages 56-57.

Materials & Tools for two trees:

- Wire trees, 10" (2)
- Acrylic paint colors: black, dark brown, dark teal, fuchsia, metallic copper, rich gold
- Sparkle glaze
- Paintbrush, 1/2" flat
- Liner brush
- Plaster of paris
- Plastic pumpkins, 3"-diameter (2)
- Adhesive spray
- Matte acrylic spray
- Hot glue gun and glue sticks
- Rhinestones, round, assorted sizes and colors
- Silk leaves
- Tweezers
- Metallic bronze floral hair

Instructions:

1. Before beginning, carefully read General Instructions on pages 4-6.
2. Position branches as desired.
3. Using a 1/2" flat brush, base-coat wire trees with dark brown.
4. Dry-brush all branches with fuchsia, then a few with metallic copper.
5. Coat all branches with sparkle glaze.
6. Mix plaster of paris according to manufacturer's directions; fill plastic pumpkins 1/2 to 3/4 full. Place trees into plaster of paris in center of plastic pumpkin.
7. Spray pumpkins with adhesive spray and allow to dry thoroughly. This must be done so the acrylic paint will adhere to the plastic.
8. Base-coat plastic pumpkins with rich gold.
9. Float-shade indentations on pumpkins (all the way around) with metallic copper.
10. Using a liner brush, paint a face on each pumpkin with black.
11. Seal paint with matte acrylic spray.
12. Randomly hot-glue rhinestones around plastic pumpkins.
13. Paint silk leaves with fuchsia, metallic copper, and dark teal.
14. Fill plastic pumpkins with metallic bronze floral hair.
15. Using tweezers, hot-glue silk leaves onto tree branches.

... using a country color scream

Photo on pages 74-75.

Materials & Tools for two trees:

- Acrylic paint colors: black, butterscotch, dark brown, light tan, metallic champagne
- Dried leaves, autumn colors
- Spanish moss

Instructions:

3. Using a 1/2" flat brush, base-coat wire trees with dark brown.
4. Dry-brush branches with butterscotch, then with light tan.
8. Mix metallic champagne and butterscotch (3:1) to make gold. Base-coat plastic pumpkins with gold.
9. Float-shade indentations on pumpkins (all the way around) with black.
10. Using a liner brush, paint a face on each pumpkin with black.
14. Fill plastic pumpkins with Spanish moss.
15. Using tweezers, hot-glue dried leaves onto tree branches and onto Spanish moss.

Buttoned Up!

Photo on pages 56-57.

Materials & Tools:

- Pipe cleaners, brown
- Round buttons, greens and blacks from 1/4" to 1 1/2"
- Wooden beads, 1/4" (for small), 1/2" (for large)

Instructions:

1. Cut pipe cleaners 3" long for small trees and 5" long for large trees.
2. Thread assorted buttons (graduating in size) on pipe cleaners. Leave at least 3/4" of pipe cleaner extending up from tops of trees.
3. Paint beads as desired.
4. Thread painted beads on pipe cleaners at tops of trees.

"Tricky" Trees

Photo on pages 56-57.

Materials & Tools for each tree:

- ◆ Braided wire, 10'
- ◆ Wire cutters
- ◆ Needlenose pliers
- ◆ Copper spray paint
- ◆ Bucket (wooden), 2" diameter x 2" high
- ◆ Wood putty
- ◆ Gesso
- ◆ Paintbrush, flat
- ◆ Acrylic paint color: dark teal
- ◆ Sparkle glaze
- ◆ Styrofoam, 2" x 2" x 1"
- ◆ Craft knife
- ◆ Hot glue gun and glue sticks
- ◆ Metallic bronze floral hair
- ◆ Balsa, 2" x 3" x $^1/_8$"
- ◆ Craft glue
- ◆ Rhinestones, round, $1^3/_4$mm clear
- ◆ See additional list of materials and tools needed for Hare Raising rabbit on page 28.

Instructions:

1. Using wire cutters, cut one piece of wire 7" long to make tree trunk.

2. Using needlenose pliers, begin bending additional wire at a right angle around top of 7" wire, forming a triangle. Repeat process, keeping 7" wire in center and gradually making triangles larger as tree is being formed. See diagram at right.

3. Spray wire tree with copper spray paint.

4. Remove wire handle from wooden bucket; use wood putty to fill holes.

5. Seal wooden bucket with gesso.

6. Using a flat brush, base-coat wooden bucket with dark teal.

7. Coat wooden bucket with sparkle glaze.

8. Using a craft knife, cut styrofoam to fit inside wooden bucket and hot-glue in place.

9. Push tree into center of styrofoam in wooden bucket and hot-glue in place.

10. Top with metallic bronze floral hair and hot-glue in place.

11. Reduce Hare Raising pattern on page 82 to 40%.

12. Follow instructions on page 28 to make a Hare Raising rabbit, using a craft knife to cut rabbit from balsa instead of pine.

13. Glue rhinestones on rabbit's collar (front only) over rich gold dots.

14. Hot-glue rabbit at a slight angle on front of wooden bucket.

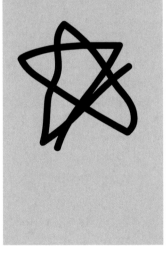

... using a country color scream

Photo on pages 74-75.

Materials & Tools:

- ♥ Acrylic paint colors: barn red, butterscotch, metallic champagne
- ♥ Spanish moss
- ♥ See additional list of materials and tools needed for Scaredy Cat on page 29.

Instructions:

6. Using a flat brush, base-coat wooden bucket $^3/_8$" up from the bottom with butterscotch, $^3/_8$" down from the top with metallic champagne, and center section with barn red.

10. Top with Spanish moss and hot-glue in place.

11. Reduce Scaredy Cat pattern on page 83 to 40%.

12. Follow instructions on page 29 to make a Scaredy Cat, using a craft knife to cut cat from balsa instead of pine.

14. Hot-glue cat at a slight angle on front of wooden bucket.

Hearth Haunts: Sunflower

Photo on page 51.

Materials & Tools:

- Pine, 8½" x 5" x ½"
- Acrylic paint color: dark blue
- Sparkle glaze
- See additional list of materials and tools needed for Spell Bloomed sunflower on page 32.

Instructions:

1. Reproduce Hearth Haunts: Sunflower #1 pattern on page 84.
2. Follow instructions on page 32 to make a Spell Bloomed sunflower.
3. Base-coat fence with black.

4. Float-shade vertical lines on fence with fuchsia.
5. Base-coat crow on top of tallest sunflower (front and back) and crows on fence (front only) with dark blue.
6. Float-shade around outside edges of all crows with black.
7. Float-highlight between crows on fence with rich gold.
8. Using a liner brush, paint crows' beaks and bird tracks up crows' bodies with rich gold.
9. Paint eyes on crows with fuchsia.
10. Paint a comma stroke onto left side of each eye with rich gold.
11. Coat fence, avoiding crows and leaves, with sparkle glaze.

... using a country color scream

Photo on pages 73.

Materials & Tools:

- ♥ Acrylic paint color: dusty purple
- ♥ See additional list of materials and tools needed for Candy Cornflower on page 33.

Instructions:

1. Reproduce Hearth Haunts: Sunflower #2 pattern on page 85.
2. Follow instructions on page 33 to make a Candy Cornflower.
3. Base-coat fence with barn red.
4. Float-shade vertical lines on fence, leaves, and stems with black.
5. Base-coat crow on top of tallest sunflower (front and back) and

crows on fence (front only) with black.
6. Float-shade around outside edges of all crows and add highlights on crows' heads and bodies with butterscotch.
7. Using a liner brush, paint crows' beaks with butterscotch.
8. Paint eyes on crows with black.
9. Paint a comma stroke onto left side of each eye with gold.
10. Mix metallic champagne and dusty purple (3:1) to make purple. Paint one square patch on crows' bodies with purple and one square patch on crows' bodies with green.
11. Paint plaid lines on purple patches with dusty purple and on green patches with forest green.
12. Paint stitches on all patches with gold.

...additional Hearth Haunts ideas

Photos on pages 56-57 & 74-75.

Instructions:

1. Use the Fowl Play, "Scare" Crow, Hare Raising, Scaredy Cat, Jack-O-Magic, and/or Country Bumpkin Pumpkin patterns on pages 82-83 and paint according to color designations given on pages 26-33 for each character.

2. Any size character(s) can be created by enlarging or reducing the appropriate patterns.

Pumpkin Patch

Photo above.

Materials & Tools:

- Papier-mâché pumpkins, various sizes
- Balsa
- Craft glue
- String of lights, optional
- Drill with ⅛" drill bit, optional
- See additional list of materials and tools needed for Trick-or-Tweet birdhouse on page 44-45.

Instructions:

1. For each building, follow instructions on pages 44-45 to make a Trick-or-Tweet bird-house. <u>Do not cut holes in front of pumpkins as doors will be painted on. Holes in bottom of pumpkins will be used for lighting if lights are desired.</u>

2. Transfer windows onto front of pumpkin using Pumpkin Patch Windows and Door patterns on page 94. Use photograph above for window placement.

3. If lighting is desired, drill two holes in each window so the light can shine through.

4. Using a craft knife, cut balsa into signs using Pumpkin Patch Signs patterns on page 94.

5. Using a black fine-point permanent marker, write names of build-ings on signs and glue them in place.

6. Buildings can be changed from simple pumpkin shapes into a variety of configurations by cutting additional papier-mâché pumpkins in half and gluing them to tops or sides of whole pumpkins. See photograph above for additional building ideas.

7. Porches can be added using twigs for porch posts and additional painted silk leaves for roofs.

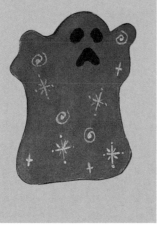

... *using a country color scream*

Photo on pages 74-75.

Materials & Tools:

♥ See additional list of materials and tools needed for Trick-or-Tweet birdhouse on page 44-46.

Instructions:

1. For each building, follow instructions on pages 44-46 to make a Trick-or-Tweet birdhouse. <u>Do not cut holes in front of pumpkins as doors will be painted on. Holes in bottom of pumpkins will be used for lighting if lights are desired.</u>

Black Jack

Photos on pages 58-59.

Materials & Tools:

✦ Transfer paper
✦ Pencil
✦ Plush felt fabric, any color (1/2 yard)
✦ Doll armatures, 3/8" (2 packages)
✦ Polyester stuffing
✦ Embroidery floss, dark pink
✦ Crewel needle, size 6
✦ Eyes (2)
✦ Ribbon (wired), any color, 1 1/2"-wide (10")
✦ Hot glue gun and glue sticks
✦ Rhinestones, small
✦ Fabric scissors
✦ Hand-sewing needle
✦ Coordinating thread
✦ Sewing machine

Instructions:

1. Enlarge Sculptured Animal patterns (for rabbit) on page 90-91 to 150%.

2. Transfer Sculptured Animal patterns (for rabbit) from page 90-91 onto plush felt fabric.

3. Using fabric scissors, cut out two fronts, two backs, one tail, and two ears from plush felt fabric.

gather stitching tight and tie off threads.

8. Form doll armature as needed and insert inside rabbit's arms and legs, according to manufacturer's directions. See diagram on page 91.

9. Using polyester stuffing, stuff rabbit.

10. Stitch tail to back at seam opening and stitch opening closed.

11. Embroider rabbit's nose and mouth with embroidery floss.

12. Add embroidery floss whiskers and sew on eyes.

13. Gather-stitch down center of ribbon and pull threads to gather. Place ribbon collar around rabbit's neck and tack ends in back to secure.

14. Randomly hot-glue rhinestones on rabbit's collar.

15. To make matching ornaments, use patterns at 100%.

4. With right sides together, machine-stitch fronts together and backs together down the centers from top of head to crotch, leaving a small opening in the back for stuffing and inserting armatures.

5. Pinch and tack end of each ear to make darts. Attach each ear to head.

6. With right sides together, machine-stitch front and back together using a ¼" seam allowance. Leave an opening in back to turn, and turn right side out.

7. Gather-stitch around rabbit's tail and pull gather stitching to form a round tail. Stuff with polyester stuffing. Pull

First skeleton: "My nose itches."
Second skeleton: "You don't have a nose."
First skeleton: "That's good because I
don't have fingernails to scratch it with!"

Jinx Minx

Photos on pages 60-61.

Materials & Tools:

♥ Transfer paper
♥ Pencil
♥ Plush felt fabric, any color (1/2 yard)
♥ Doll armatures, 3/8" (2 packages)
♥ Polyester stuffing
♥ Embroidery floss, light pink
♥ Crewel needle, size 6
♥ Eyes (2)
♥ Pastel chalk
♥ Fabric scissors
♥ Hand-sewing needle
♥ Coordinating thread
♥ Sewing machine

Instructions:

1. Enlarge Sculptured Animal patterns (for cat) on pages 90-91 to 150%.

2. Transfer Sculptured Animal patterns (for cat) from pages 90-91 onto plush felt fabric.

3. Using fabric scissors, cut out two fronts, two backs, one tail, and ears from plush felt fabric.

4. With right sides together, machine-stitch fronts together and backs together down the centers from top of head to crotch, leaving a small opening in the back for stuffing and inserting armatures.

Roasted Pumpkin Seeds

Not shown.

✦ Pumpkin seeds
✦ Melted butter (unsalted)
✦ Vegetable spray
✦ Salt

✦ Preheat oven to 350° F. Rinse pumpkin seeds well. For every 2 cups of seeds, place 4 cups of water and 2 tablespoons of salt into a saucepan. Add seeds and simmer over low heat for 10 minutes. Drain well. Place seeds on paper towels and pat dry. For every 2 cups of seeds, toss with 1 tablespoon melted, unsalted butter in a large bowl until seeds are evenly coated. Spray a cookie sheet with vegetable spray. Spread seeds on cookie sheet and bake for 30 minutes, stirring and tossing occasionally. Seeds are ready when golden brown.

Crow Cookies

Photo on page 68.

✦ 1½ c. confectioner's sugar
✦ 1 c. butter or margarine
✦ 1 tsp. baking soda
✦ 1 tsp. cream of tartar
✦ ½ tsp. almond extract
✦ 2½ c. flour
✦ 1 egg
✦ 1 tsp. vanilla
✦ Candy eyes
✦ Black shoelace licorice

✦ Combine first eight ingredients together in a large mixing bowl. Stir until thoroughly mixed and refrigerate for 2 to 3 hours. While cookie dough is chilling, make a crow-shaped cookie cutter by tracing Crow Cookie Cutter pattern on page 88 onto a disposable plastic lid (such as one from a tub of margarine). Cut crow shape out. Using a rolling pin, roll out chilled cookie dough to ¼" thickness. Dip plastic crow-shaped cookie cutter into flour and place it on top of cookie dough. Using a paring knife, cut around crow shape. Repeat process until all cookie dough has been used. Mold edges of each crow cookie so they are smooth. Using a broken toothpick, poke holes in bottom of crow to accommodate crow's legs. Bake at 375° F for 7 to 8 minutes. Allow cookies to cool and frost.

✦ Embellish each crow cookie with candy eyes and use shoelace licorice to make crow's legs. Cut each piece of licorice in half and thread it through holes in bottom of crows.

5. Pinch and tack end of each ear to make darts. Attach each ear to head.

6. With right sides together, machine-stitch front and back together using a ¼" seam allowance. Leave an opening in back to turn, and turn right side out.

7. Fold tail in half and machine-stitch together using a ¼" seam allowance. Turn right side out.

8. Form doll armature as needed and insert inside cat's arms, legs, and tail, according to manufacturer's directions. See diagram on page 91.

9. Using polyester stuffing, stuff cat.

10. Stitch tail to back at seam opening and stitch opening closed.

11. Embroider cat's nose and mouth with embroidery floss.

12. Add embroidery floss whiskers and sew on eyes.

13. If using light colored plush felt fabric, highlight around cat's eyes using pastel chalk.

14. To make matching ornaments, use patterns at 100%.

Abra Cadabra!

Photo on page 62.

Materials & Tools:

- Balls with flat bottoms (wooden), 2½" diameter (2)
- Candle cups (wooden), 1⅜" diameter (2)
- Wooden dowels, ³⁄₁₆" diameter x 1" length (2)
- Drill with ³⁄₁₆" drill bit
- Paintbrush, ¼" flat
- Liner brush
- Acrylic paint color: antique copper
- Matte acrylic spray
- Craft glue
- Rhinestones, round, 3mm assorted colors
- Wood glue
- Tapered candles (2)
- See additional list of materials and tools needed for Crows' Feet crows on page 42.

Instructions:

1. Reproduce Fowl Play pattern (without legs) on page 82 at 100%.

2. Follow instructions on page 42 to make two Crows' Feet crows. <u>Do not allow pine for crows' legs, as crows' legs should not be cut out.</u>

3. Drill one ½" hole centered in bottom of each crow and in top of each ball to accommodate wooden dowels.

4. Seal balls and candle cups with gesso.

5. Using a ¼" flat brush, base-coat balls with rich gold.

6. Float-shade indentations on pumpkins (all the way around) with antique copper.

7. Using a liner brush, paint a face on each pumpkin with black.

8. Base-coat candle cups with fuchsia.

9. Paint bird tracks across candle cups with rich gold.

10. Seal paint with matte acrylic spray.

11. Glue rhinestones around top edges of candle cups.

12. Glue wooden dowels into drilled holes in bottom of crows and in top of balls. Push crows down onto balls so wooden dowels cannot be seen.

13. Glue candle cups centered to tops of crows' heads.

14. Place tapered candles into candle cups so they are secure.

Gelatin Wigglers

Photo on page 67.

- 6 4-oz. pkgs. gelatin: 2 each of grape, pineapple, and cranberry
- Colored candy

- Make each gelatin flavor separately according to package directions. When set, cut gelatin into diamond shapes. To remove gelatin diamonds, place pans in hot water for approximately 15 seconds to loosen edges. Arrange gelatin diamonds in a harlequin pattern on a serving platter and place one colored candy between each gelatin diamond.

... using a country color scream

Photo on page 77.

Materials & Tools:

- See additional list of materials and tools needed for Crows' Feet crows on page 42.

Instructions:

1. Reproduce "Scare" Crow pattern (without legs) on page 82 at 100%.

2. Follow instructions on page 42 to make two Crows' Feet crows.

5. Using a ¼" flat brush, base-coat balls with gold.

6. Float-shade indentations on pumpkins (all the way around) with black.

7. Using a liner brush, paint eyes and a mouth on each pumpkin with black. Paint a candy corn nose on each pumpkin with butterscotch, barn red, and metallic champagne.

8. Base-coat candle cups with purple.

9. Paint vertical and horizontal lines on candle cups (all the way around) with dusty purple.

Haunted House

Photo on page 62.

Materials & Tools:

- Birch plywood,
  2' x 4' x ¹/₄"
- Pine, 2" x 6" x ¹/₂"
- Transfer paper
- Pencil
- Table saw
- Jigsaw
- Scroll saw
- Sandpaper
- Gesso
- Wood glue
- Ruler
- Craft knife
- Jumbo craft sticks,
  6" (40)
- Balsa, ¹/₂" x 5³/₈"
  x ¹/₈"-thick
- Paper twist ribbon,
  dark green (1 pkg.)
- Craft scissors
- Craft glue
- Paintbrushes, flat
- Paintbrushes, round
- Liner brush
- Acrylic paint colors:
  antique copper,
  black, butterscotch,
  dark teal, emerald
  green, fuchsia,
  light gray, metallic
  champagne, metallic
  gold, purple, rich
  brown
- Sparkle glaze
- Balsa, 3" x 6"
  x ¹/₄"-thick
- Wooden dowels,
  ¹/₄" diameter x
  8" length (2)
- Balsa, 1¹/₄" x 3¹/₄"
  x ¹/₄"-thick (2)
- Balsa, ¹/₄" x 18¹/₂"
  x ¹/₈"-thick
- Toothpicks, flat (30)
- Push pin
- Wire cutters
- Wire, 16-gauge
- Needlenose pliers
- Hot glue gun and
  glue sticks
- Old toothbrush
- Rhinestones, round,
  3mm assorted colors
- Matte acrylic spray

Instructions:

1. Before beginning, carefully read General Instructions on pages 4-6.

2. Enlarge Haunted House patterns on pages 92-93 to 168%.

3. Transfer Haunted House patterns from pages 92-93 onto birch plywood.

4. Transfer Moon and Pumpkin patterns from page 94 onto pine.

5. Using a table saw, cut all shapes from plywood.

6. Using a jigsaw, cut out windows.

7. Using a scroll saw, cut one moon and three pumpkins from pine.

8. Sand plywood as necessary and seal with gesso.

9. Seal pine with gesso.

10. Using wood glue, assemble all four house walls. Glue house and widow's walk roofs together. Do not glue roofs or base on at this time.

11. Using a craft knife, cut 1¹/₄" off each end of jumbo craft sticks to make shingles.

12. Set aside center sections of jumbo craft sticks to make shutters.

13. Beginning along bottom edge of roof line for house roof, glue shingles into position. Trim excess.

14. Carve small nicks along one long edge of ¹/₈"-thick (x ¹/₂" x 5³/₈") balsa to make roof ridge moulding and glue in place.

15. Measure height of house and cut paper twist ribbon to fit. Untwist ribbon, but

do not smooth it out completely as the wrinkled and raised texture is desired.

16. Using craft glue, adhere the pieces of paper twist ribbon to outside walls, working left to right, one wall at a time. Slightly overlap seams and cover all windows.

17. Trim excess ribbon and cut out windows.

18. Using a flat brush, paint paper twist ribbon on haunted house with black. It is not necessary to get paint into all crevices.

19. Paint shingles and roof ridge moulding on house roof and paint widow's walk roof with black.

20. Wash shingles on house roof and sponge-paint widow's walk roof with emerald green, then with light gray.

21. Cut ¹/₄"-thick balsa into two 1¹/₂" x 6" pieces to make porch roofs.

22. Cut both wooden dowels in half to make porch posts.

23. Using a craft knife, cut $1/8$"-thick balsa into thirteen $1/4$" x $1^{1}/_{16}$" pieces to make window ledges for vertical windows. Cut two $1/4$" x $2^{1}/_{4}$" pieces to make window ledges for horizontal windows.

24. Paint porch roofs, porch posts, base, window ledges, and toothpicks with black.

25. Wash haunted house, porch roofs, porch posts, base, window ledges, and toothpicks with light gray.

26. Cut center sections of each jumbo craft stick into two pieces to make shutters. Trim four of the pieces to $1^{1}/_{4}$" in height for shutters on horizontal windows. Paint twelve shutters, including the four that are $1^{1}/_{4}$" high, with fuchsia. Paint eight shutters with dark teal.

27. Using a round brush, paint diamonds on doors (front and back). Paint half the diamonds with dark teal and remaining diamonds with purple.

28. Wash all shutters and both doors with black.

29. Lightly sand edges of shingles and roof ridge moulding on house roof, widow's walk roof, porch roofs, window ledges, base, all shutters, and both doors to randomly remove some paint for a weathered appearance.

30. Using a liner brush, randomly paint swirls and stars on all shutters using Swirls and Stars patterns on page 94 and outline all diamonds on doors (front and back) with metallic gold.

31. Paint door knobs on doors with black.

32. Using a flat brush, base-coat moon (front and back) with metallic champagne.

33. Mix metallic champagne and butterscotch (3:1) to make gold. Base-coat pumpkins with gold.

34. Float-shade indentations on pumpkins (fronts and backs) with antique copper.

35. Paint pumpkin stems with rich brown.

36. Lightly sand edges of moon and pumpkins to randomly remove some paint for a weathered appearance.

37. Punch eight holes spaced 1" apart on top of widow's walk roof and one hole in center of house roof (one side only) with a push pin to accommodate wires.

38. Using wire cutters, cut eight $1^{1}/_{2}$" pieces, one 24" piece, and one 6" piece from 16-gauge wire.

39. Using needlenose pliers, push $1^{1}/_{2}$" pieces of wire into holes on top of widow's walk roof and bend each end to form a loop.

40. Thread 24" piece of wire through loops and secure ends to make a balcony on widow's walk roof.

41. Spiral 6" piece of wire and push into hole in center of house roof.

42. Using a hot glue gun and glue sticks, adhere toothpicks inside windows to make cross members.

Hot-glue vertical cross members first, then horizontal ones.

43. Hot-glue window ledges, window shutters, and doors in place.

44. Using wood glue, glue house to base and glue both roofs on.

45. Glue porch roofs onto sides of house above windows and doors. Carefully place porch posts into position and glue to secure.

46. Using an old toothbrush, fly-speck each side of haunted house and moon and pumpkins with the following colors: antique copper, emerald green, fuchsia, metallic gold, and purple.

47. Punch one hole into one end of moon with a push pin to accommodate wire.

48. Place wire in center of house roof into hole in end of moon; secure with industrial-strength glue.

49. Glue pumpkins onto porch roofs.

50. Coat shingles, moon, and pumpkins with sparkle glaze.

51. Seal paint with matte acrylic spray.

52. Glue three rhinestones over swirls and stars on each dark teal-colored shutter.

... *using a country color scream*

Photo on page 78.

Materials & Tools:

♥ Acrylic paint colors: antique copper, barn red, black, butterscotch, dusty purple, emerald green, forest green, light gray, metallic champagne, rich brown

Instructions:

26. Cut center sections of each jumbo craft stick into two pieces to make shutters. Trim four of the pieces to 1¹/₄" in height for shutters on horizontal windows. Paint twelve shutters, including the four that are 1¹/₄" high, with barn red. Mix metallic champagne and dusty purple (3:1) to make purple. Paint eight shutters with purple.

27. Mix metallic champagne and butterscotch (3:1) to make gold. Base-coat doors with gold. Using a round brush, paint candy corn on doors (front and back) using Candy Corn pattern on page 94 with butterscotch, barn red, and metallic champagne.

30. Using a liner brush, randomly paint vertical lines on all shutters with metallic champagne and horizontal lines on all shutters with black.

33. Base-coat pumpkins with gold.

46. Using an old toothbrush, fly-speck each side of haunted house and moon and pumpkins with the following colors: barn red, forest green, gold, and purple.

Poison Apples

Photos on pages 67 & 77.

Materials & Tools:

◆ Transfer paper
◆ Pencil
◆ Fabric, ¹/₂ yard
◆ Fabric scissors
◆ Coordinating thread
◆ Sewing machine
◆ Gold cording or Twine
◆ Halloween candies
◆ Twigs (10)

Instructions:

1. Enlarge Poison Apple Treat Bag pattern on page 90 to 135%.

2. Transfer Poison Apple Treat Bag pattern from page 90 onto fabric ten times.

3. Double fabric and cut ten treat bags.

4. To make casing, fold top of fabric down ¹/₄", then fold down another ¹/₄".

5. Machine-stitch along inside top edge. With right sides together, match fronts to backs.

6. Machine-stitch around sides and bottom. Do not stitch casing closed.

7. Open bag in opposite direction and machine-stitch seam across ¹/₄" of side seam to make a gusset. Repeat process for other side of bag.

8. Thread gold cording or twine through the casings of each bag.

9. Fill the bags with Halloween candies.

10. Insert a twig into each bag and pull the cording or twine in opposite directions to close bags.

11. Wrap cording or twine around bags to look like apples and tie at top.

Beefed Up Buns

Photo above.

- ✦ 1½ lbs. lean ground beef
- ✦ ½ c. chopped onion
- ✦ ¼ tsp. oregano
- ✦ ½ tsp. salt
- ✦ ½ tsp. seasoned salt
- ✦ ⅛ tsp. garlic powder
- ✦ ½ c. brown sugar
- ✦ 1 tsp. prepared mustard
- ✦ 1 8-oz. can tomato sauce
- ✦ Hamburger buns
- ✦ Orange food spray
- ✦ 1 4-oz. pkg. cream cheese
- ✦ 1 tsp. milk
- ✦ Cake decorating paste, concentrated: black and brown

✦ In a large skillet, combine ground beef and chopped onion and cook over medium heat until ground beef is browned. Add next seven ingredients to skillet. Mix well and allow to simmer until hot. Using a sharp knife, remove strips from the top of each hamburger bun. Spray hamburger buns with orange food spray to resemble pumpkins. Mix cream cheese and milk until smooth. Add black cake decorating paste to mixture for desired color. A hint of brown cake decorating paste must be added so the black does not turn purple. Place mixture into a frosting bag and, using a cake decorating tip, draw a face on the top of each hamburger bun. Put hot hamburger mixture inside buns and serve.

Cranberry Cider

Photo above.

- ✦ 1 pkg. fresh cranberries
- ✦ 3 qts. water
- ✦ 2 cinnamon sticks
- ✦ 9 whole cloves
- ✦ 1½ c. sugar
- ✦ ½ c. orange juice
- ✦ ¼ c. lemon juice

✦ Combine first four ingredients in large saucepan. Bring to boil, cover, and simmer for 25 minutes. Strain and discard cranberry pulp, cinnamon sticks, and whole cloves. Immediately add sugar, orange juice, and lemon juice and stir until sugar is dissolved. Pour into a punch bowl and serve hot or allow to cool and serve over ice. Makes 3 quarts.

Is it true that witches
are not afraid
of dead bodies?

Of corpse!

Kooky Bucket

Photo above.

Materials & Tools:

- Octagon bucket (wooden), 7³/₄" high
- Paintbrush, ¹/₂" flat
- Gesso
- Acrylic paint colors: black, dark teal, emerald green, fuchsia
- Pinecones
- Sparkle glaze
- Clothesline wire
- Pliers
- Matte acrylic spray
- Industrial-strength glue
- Clamps
- Craft glue, optional
- Rhinestones, round, assorted sizes and colors, optional
- See additional lists of materials and tools needed for Fowl Play crow on page 26, Hare Raising rabbit on page 28, and Jack-O-Magic on page 30.

Instructions:

1. Before beginning, carefully read General Instructions on pages 4-6.

2. Remove handle.

3. Seal wooden bucket (inside and out) with gesso.

4. Using a ¹/₂" flat brush, base-coat wooden bucket (inside and out) with black.

5. Dip a pinecone in dark teal and roll it over entire outside and top edge of wooden bucket to make a pattern.

6. Using another pinecone, repeat process with emerald green.

7. Using another pinecone, repeat process with fuchsia.

8. Coat bucket with sparkle glaze.

9. Use clothesline wire to make a new handle

by bending it to form the word "treats." Use pliers on areas that need to be crimped into shape.

10. Coat handle with sparkle glaze.

11. Hook formed handle onto wooden bucket; crimp with pliers to secure.

12. Seal paint with matte acrylic spray.

13. Reduce Fowl Play pattern on page 82 to 85%.

14. Enlarge Hare Raising pattern on page 82 to 105%.

15. Enlarge Jack-O-Magic pattern on page 83 to 105%.

16. Follow instructions on page 26 to make two Fowl Play crows.

17. Follow instructions on page 28 to make two Hare Raising rabbits.

18. Follow instructions on page 30 to make two Jack-O-Magics.

19. Glue characters onto sides of bucket, aligning bottoms.

20. Clamp characters in position until glue has thoroughly dried.

21. If desired, glue a rhinestone in the center of each swirl and star on bottom pumpkins, on snowmens' hats over metallic gold dots and fuchsia diamonds, and on rabbits' collars over rich gold dots.

... *using a country color scream*

Photo below.

Materials & Tools:

♥ Fruit basket, 8" diameter
♥ Acrylic paint colors: barn red, butterscotch, metallic champagne
♥ Black spray paint
♥ See additional lists of materials and tools needed for "Scare" Crow on page 27, Scaredy Cat on page 29, and Country Bumpkin Pumpkin on page 31.

Instructions:

3. Seal fruit basket (inside and out) with gesso.

4. Using a 1/2" flat brush, base-coat fruit basket (inside, except top rim) with barn red.

5. Paint bottom section of fruit basket (outside) with metallic champagne.

6. Paint middle section of fruit basket (outside) with barn red.

7. Mix metallic champagne and butterscotch (3:1) to make gold. Paint top rim of fruit basket (inside and out) with gold.

10. Spray handle with black spray paint.

11. Hook formed handle onto fruit basket; crimp with pliers to secure.

13. Reduce "Scare" Crow pattern on page 82 to 85%.

14. Reduce Scaredy Cat pattern on page 83 to 95%.

15. Reduce Country Bumpkin Pumpkin pattern on page 83 to 95%.

16. Follow instructions on page 27 to make two "Scare" Crows.

17. Follow instructions on page 29 to make two Scaredy Cats.

18. Follow instructions on page 31 to make two Country Bumpkin Pumpkins.

19. Glue characters onto sides of basket, aligning bottoms.

Mystical Brew

Photo on page 67.

Materials & Tools:

- ✦ Bubble ball, 10"
- ✦ Wine glasses
- ✦ Fine-point permanent marker, metallic gold
- ✦ Medium-point permanent marker, metallic gold
- ✦ Industrial-strength glue
- ✦ Rhinestones, round, assorted sizes and colors
- ✦ Craft scissors
- ✦ Mesh ribbon (wired), metallic gold, $1/2$"-wide

Instructions:

1. Using metallic gold markers, randomly draw swirls and stars onto bubble ball (for punch bowl) and wine glasses using Swirls and Stars patterns on page 94.

2. Glue a rhinestone in the center of each swirl and star on bubble ball and on wine glasses.

3. Cut mesh ribbon into 15" lengths and tie around stems of wine glasses. Spiral one end of each ribbon up each stem and spiral the other ends outward.

Scary Scoop

Photo on page 67.

Materials & Tools:

- ✦ Plastic ladle
- ✦ Beads, assorted sizes and colors
- ✦ Gold wire, 28-gauge
- ✦ Dremel tool

Instructions:

1. Using a dremel tool, drill one hole into top of ladle handle, two on the left side, and two on the right side.

2. Thread 28-gauge wire through hole in top of handle and twist to keep beads from falling off.

3. Add beads onto wire while threading wire through remaining drilled holes. At the last hole, add several beads and twist wire to keep beads from falling off.

Bat's Vat

Photo on page 77.

Materials & Tools:

- ♥ Plastic cauldron, black, 11" diameter x $8^1/2$" high
- ♥ Plastic glasses
- ♥ Paintbrushes, flat
- ♥ Liner brush
- ♥ Acrylic paint colors: barn red, black, butterscotch, forest green, metallic champagne, rich brown
- ♥ Liquid varnish

Instructions:

1. Before beginning, carefully read General Instructions on pages 4-6.

2. Mix metallic champagne and butterscotch (3:1) to make gold. Base-coat pumpkins on plastic glasses with gold.

3. Float-shade indentations on pumpkins with black.

4. Using a liner brush, paint eyes and a mouth on each pumpkin with black.

5. Paint a candy corn nose on each pumpkin with butterscotch, barn red, and metallic champagne.

6. Paint a stem on each pumpkin with rich brown.

7. Mix metallic champagne and forest green (3:1) to make green. Paint a vine with leaves on each pumpkin with green.

8. Seal paint with liquid varnish.

Spider Spoon

Photo on page 77.

Materials & Tools:

- ♥ Plastic ladle
- ♥ Spider
- ♥ Artificial spider web
- ♥ Hot glue gun and glue sticks

Instructions:

1. Wrap artificial spider web on spider's legs.

2. Hot-glue onto ladle handle.

Country Hocus Pocus

Chocolate Scaredy Snacks

Not shown.

- ♥ 3 tbsp. margarine
- ♥ 10 oz. pkg. marshmallows
- ♥ 6 c. krispie rice cereal
- ♥ Vegetable spray
- ♥ 1 c. chocolate chips
- ♥ Orange candy sprinkles

♥ Melt margarine in a large saucepan over low heat. Add marshmallows and stir until completely melted. Remove from heat. Add krispie rice cereal and stir until well coated. Using ¹/₂ cup measuring cup coated with vegetable spray, portion warm krispie rice mixture and firmly shape into round balls. Insert a popsicle stick in the center of each ball. Melt chocolate chips in a small saucepan over low heat and dip the bottom of each ball into melted chocolate. Decorate each ball with candy sprinkles. Refrigerate until chocolate is firm. Makes 12 balls.

Snack-O-Lanterns

Not shown.

- ♥ 3 tbsp. margarine
- ♥ 10 oz. pkg. marshmallows
- ♥ 6 c. krispie rice cereal
- ♥ Vegetable spray
- ♥ Orange decorating gel

♥ Melt margarine in a large saucepan over low heat. Add marshmallows and stir until completely melted. Remove from heat. Add krispie rice cereal and stir until well coated. Coat 13 x 9 x 2 pan with vegetable spray and press krispie rice mixture evenly into pan. When mixture has slightly cooled, cut into circles using a 3-inch round cookie cutter. Using orange decorating gel, decorate each treat with a pumpkin face. Makes 12 snack-o-lanterns.

Sherbet Jack-O-Lanterns

Not shown.

♥ Fresh oranges
♥ Orange sherbet
♥ Permanent marker, black

♥ Cut the tops off each fresh orange and remove the pulp from inside each orange using a spoon. Rinse and allow outsides of oranges to dry thoroughly — about 15 minutes. Using a black permanent marker, draw a jack-o-lantern face on each orange. Fill each orange with orange sherbet and place in freezer until sherbet is frozen.

Dirt Dessert

Photo on pages 77-78.

♥ Cream-filled chocolate cookies   ♥ Gummy worms
♥ Chocolate or vanilla ice cream

♥ Using a butter knife, scrape cream centers from chocolate cookies. Using a rolling pin, roll chocolate cookies into crumbs to make dirt. Place chocolate cookie crumbs into the bottom of each serving dish, reserving some crumbs. Using a large spoon, scoop ice cream from carton and place in serving dishes. Sprinkle reserved cookie crumbs on top of ice cream and place in freezer to set. Just before serving, place gummy worms in the dessert so they appear to be crawling out of the dirt.

Dinner In A Pumpkin

Photo on page 77.

- ♥ Med.-sized pumpkin (4 lbs.)
- ♥ 1¹/₂ lbs. lean ground beef
- ♥ ¹/₃ c. chopped green pepper
- ♥ ³/₄ c. chopped celery
- ♥ ³/₄ c. chopped onion
- ♥ 1 tsp. salt
- ♥ ¹/₄ tsp. pepper
- ♥ ¹/₄ c. soy sauce
- ♥ 2 tbsp. brown sugar
- ♥ 1 4-oz. can mushrooms
- ♥ 1 can cr. of chicken soup
- ♥ 2 c. cooked rice
- ♥ Black olives
- ♥ Steamed carrot
- ♥ Whole cloves
- ♥ Fresh parsley leaves

♥ Using a sharp knife, cut lid from pumpkin and scoop out pumpkin seeds and excess membrane with a scraping tool. In a large skillet, combine ground beef, chopped green pepper, chopped celery, and chopped onion and cook over medium heat until ground beef is browned. Add next seven ingredients to skillet. Mix well and place mixture into pumpkin cavity. Place lid on pumpkin. Place pumpkin on a foil-lined cookie sheet and bake at 350° F for 1¹/₂ hours. Just before serving, embellish pumpkin by placing (with toothpicks) black olives to make eyes, a steamed carrot to make a nose, and whole cloves to make a mouth. Use fresh parsley leaves to make hair around lid opening. To serve, scoop out part of the baked pumpkin, along with the meat mixture, onto each plate.

Ghoul-Aid

Photo on page 77.

- ♥ 1 pkg. grape powdered fruit drink
- ♥ 1 pkg. orange powdered fruit drink
- ♥ 2 c. sugar
- ♥ 3 qts. cold water
- ♥ 1 qt. ginger ale

♥ Combine both powdered fruit drink flavors in a pitcher and make according to package directions. Add ginger ale and stir to mix well. Pour into a punch bowl and serve over ice. This punch is as black as midnight and is frightfully delicious!

*How do ghosts
get to
the second
floor?*

*They take
the scares!*

Great
Bags of
Fire

TRICK

OR

TREAT

Great
Bags of
Fire

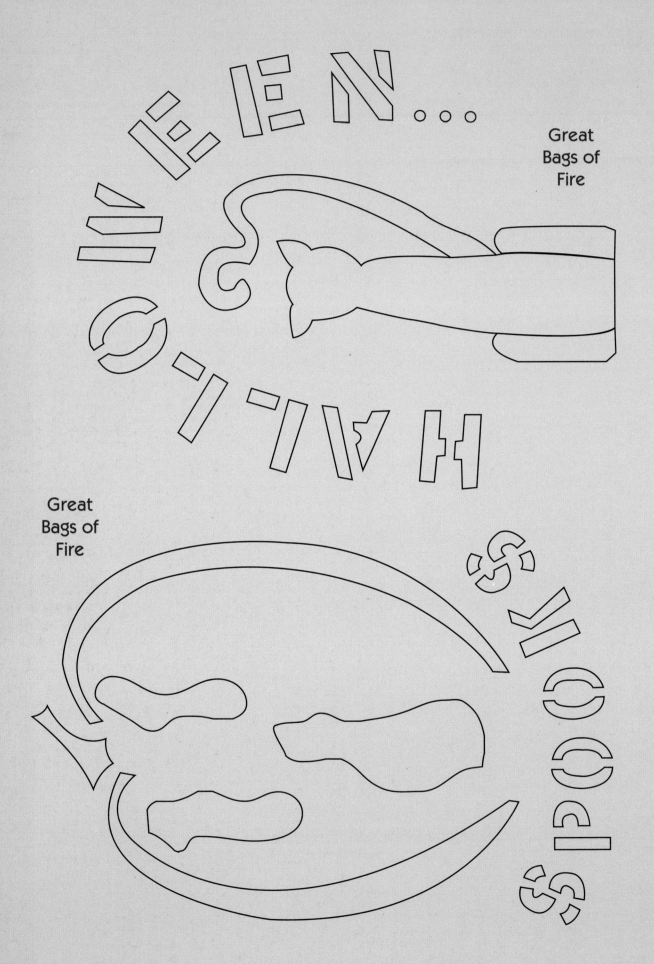

Great
Bags of
Fire

Great
Bags of
Fire

Spooks'
Night
Out

SPOOKS' NIGHT OUT

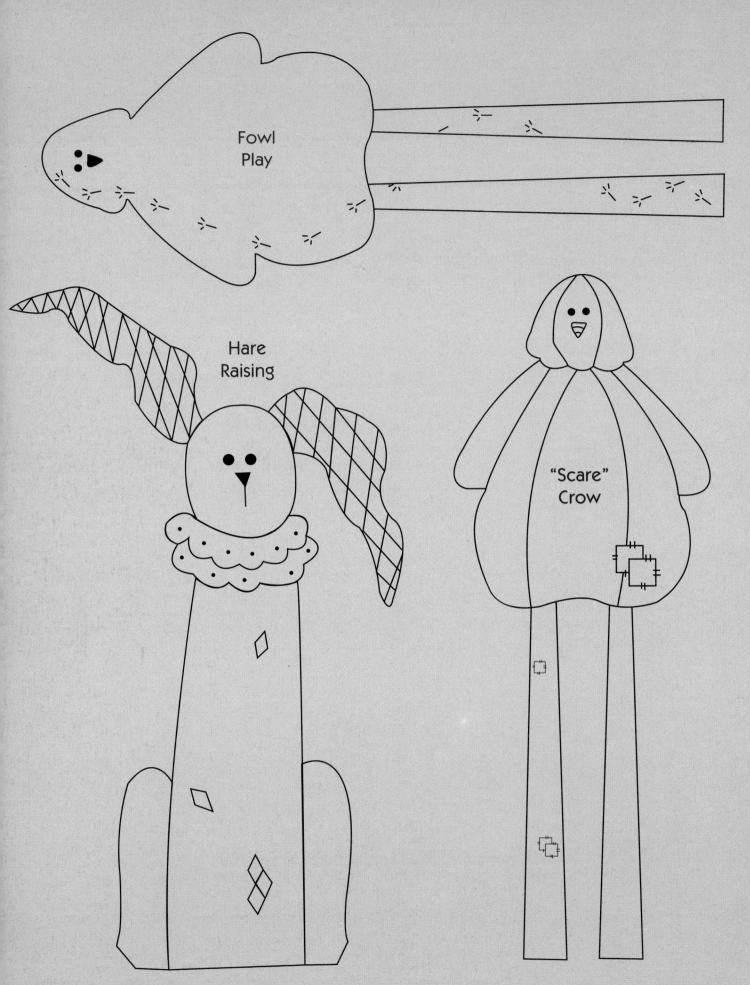

Fowl
Play

Hare
Raising

"Scare"
Crow

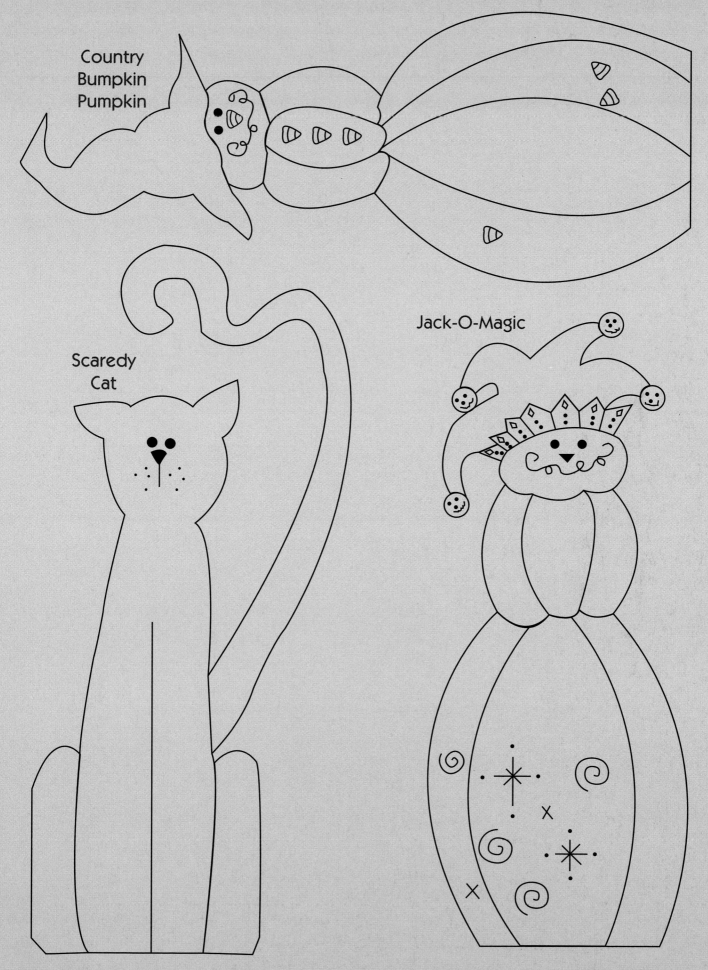

Country
Bumpkin
Pumpkin

Jack-O-Magic

Scaredy
Cat

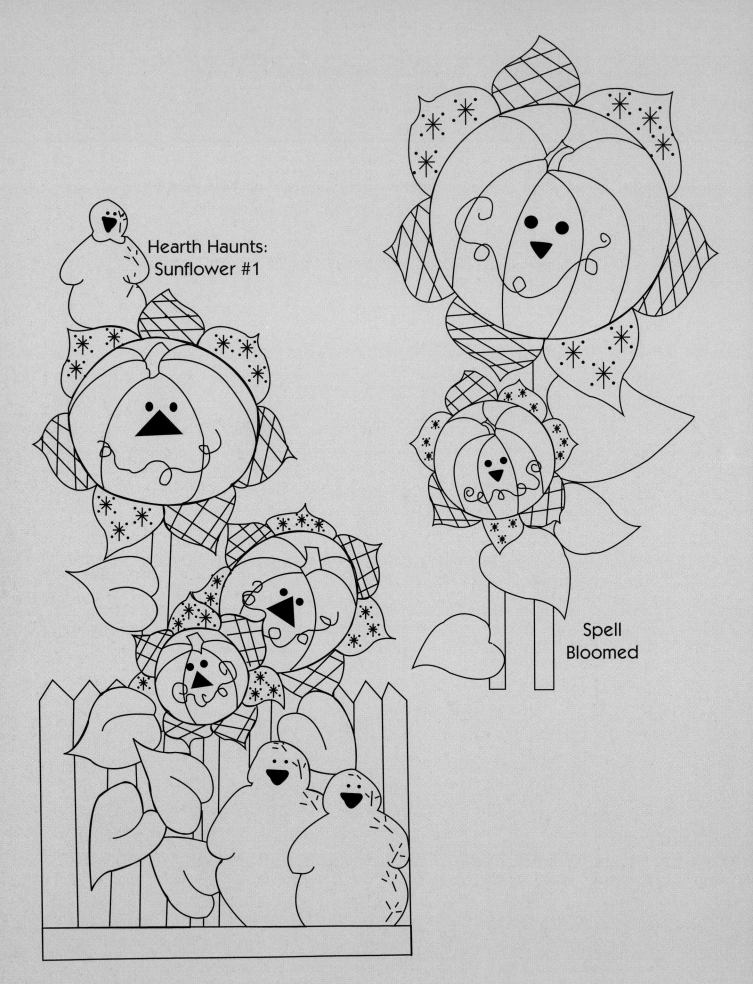

Hearth Haunts:
Sunflower #1

Spell
Bloomed

Hearth Haunts:
Sunflower #2

Candy
Cornflower

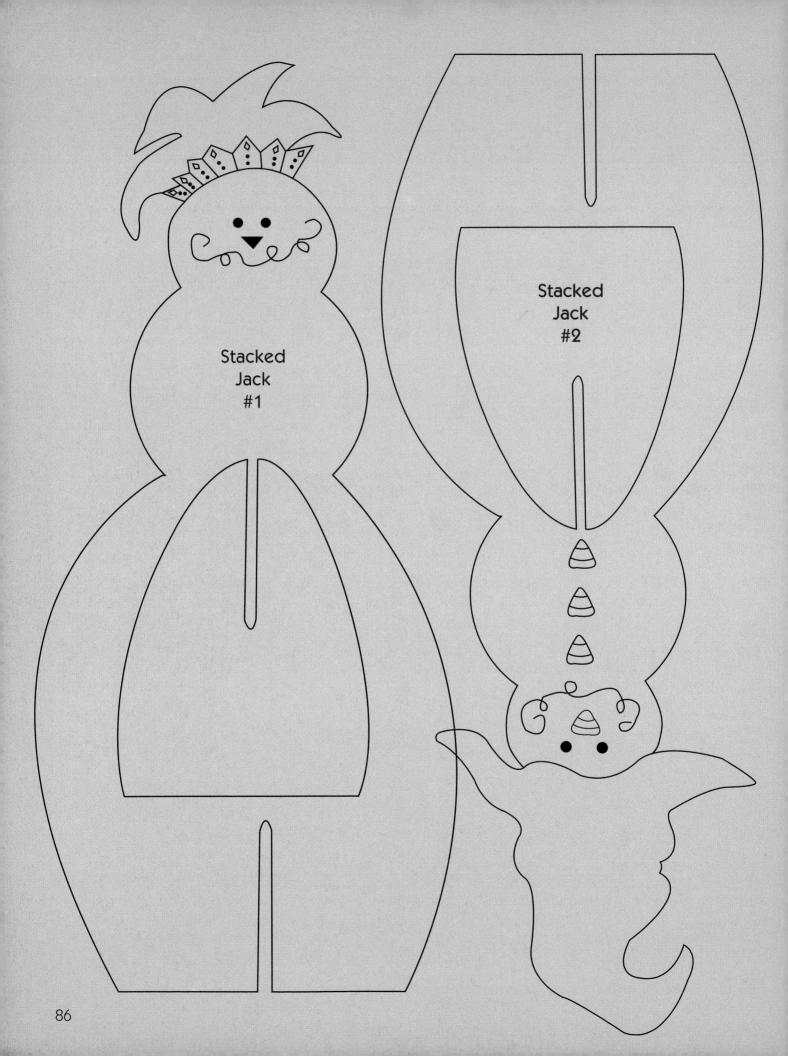

Stacked
Jack
#1

Stacked
Jack
#2

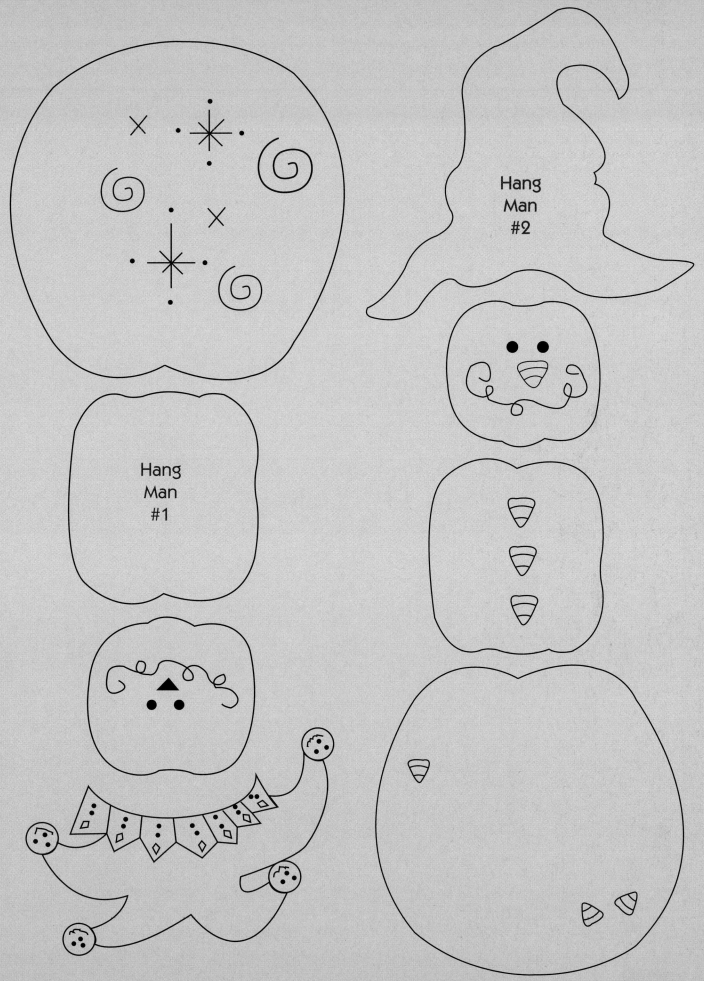

Hang
Man
#1

Hang
Man
#2

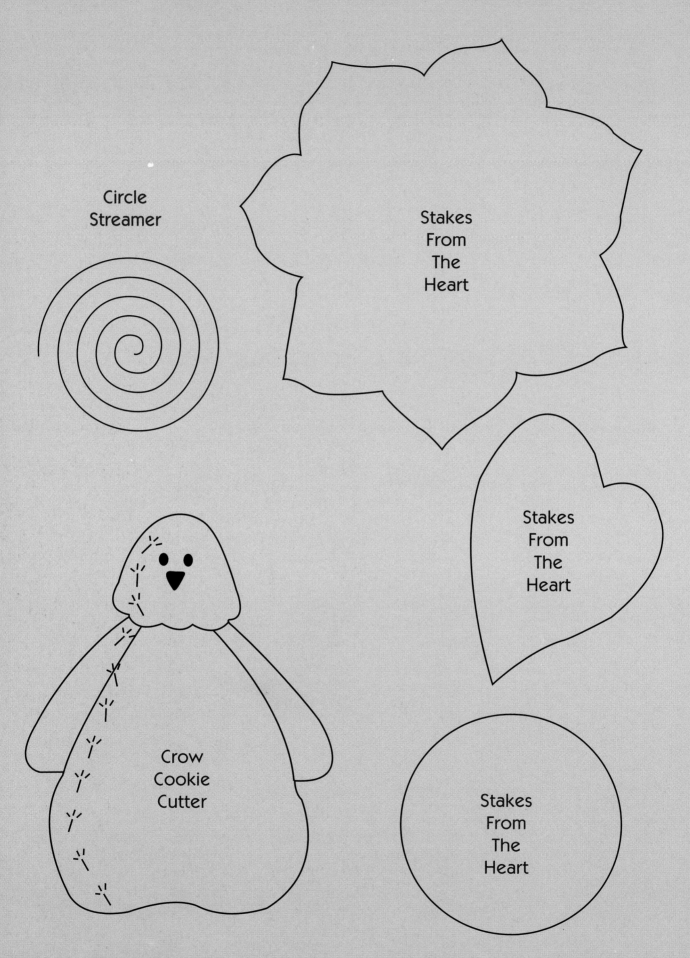

Circle
Streamer

Stakes
From
The
Heart

Stakes
From
The
Heart

Crow
Cookie
Cutter

Stakes
From
The
Heart

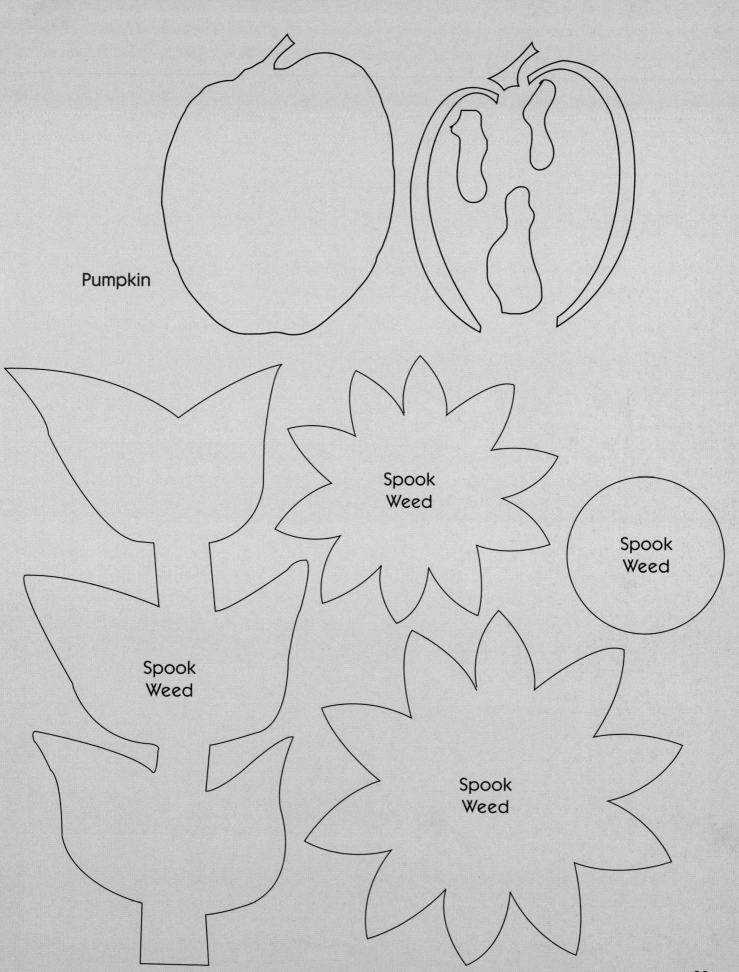

Pumpkin

Spook
Weed

Spook
Weed

Spook
Weed

Spook
Weed

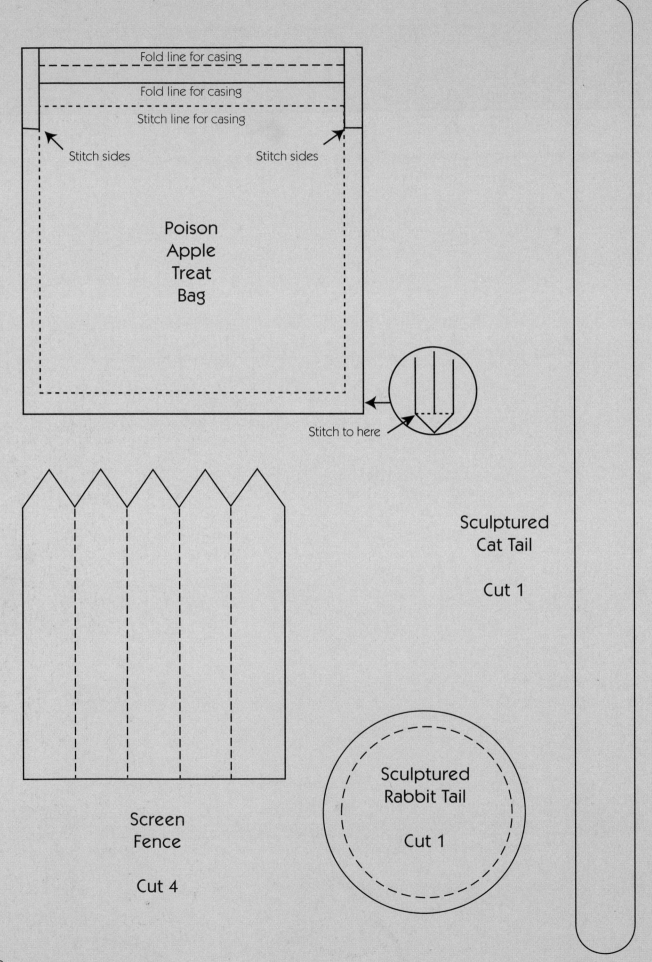

Fold line for casing

Fold line for casing

Stitch line for casing

Stitch sides   Stitch sides

Poison
Apple
Treat
Bag

Stitch to here

Sculptured
Cat Tail

Cut 1

Sculptured
Rabbit Tail

Cut 1

Screen
Fence

Cut 4

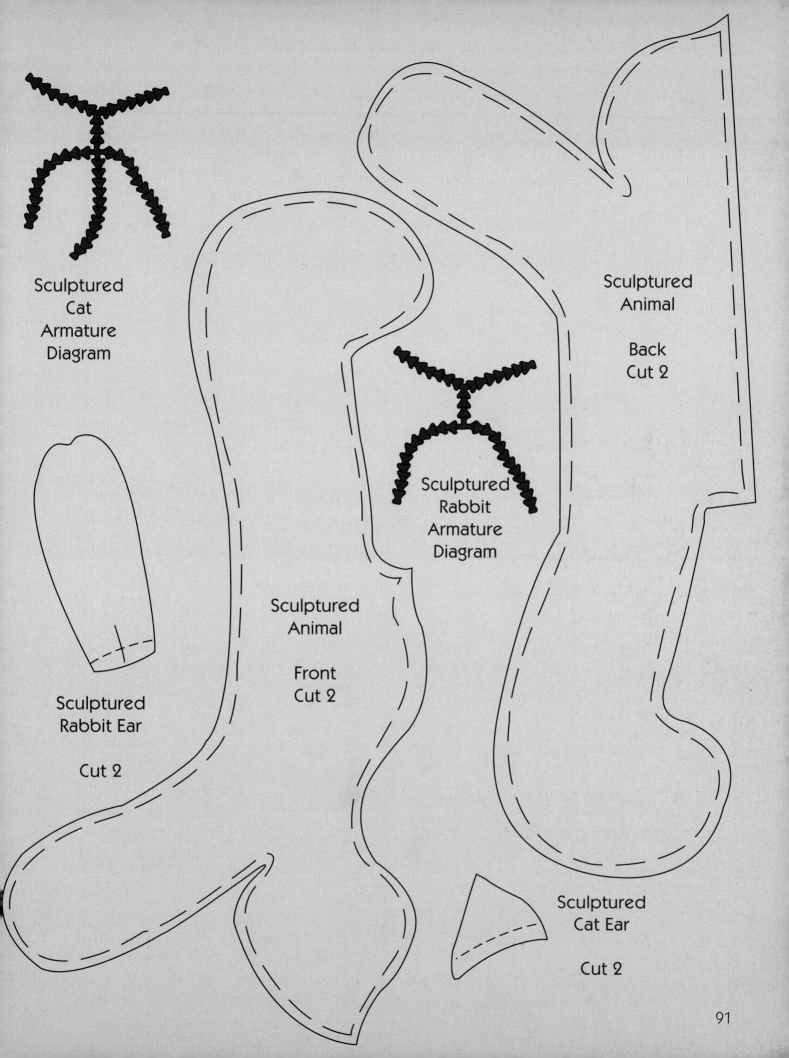

Sculptured
Cat
Armature
Diagram

Sculptured
Animal

Back
Cut 2

Sculptured
Rabbit
Armature
Diagram

Sculptured
Rabbit Ear

Cut 2

Sculptured
Animal

Front
Cut 2

Sculptured
Cat Ear

Cut 2

91

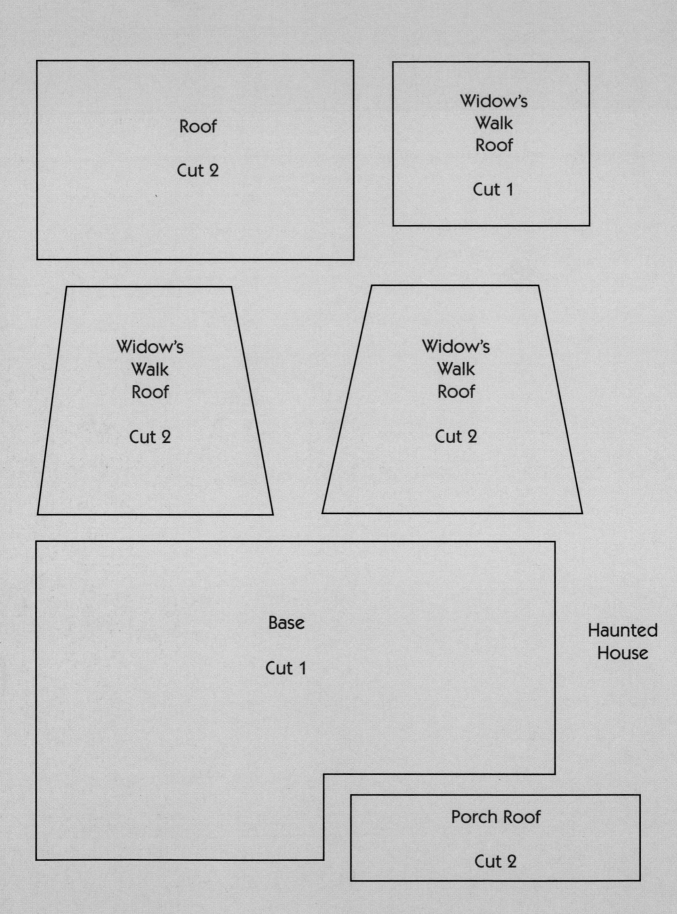

Roof

Cut 2

Widow's Walk Roof

Cut 1

Widow's Walk Roof

Cut 2

Widow's Walk Roof

Cut 2

Base

Cut 1

Haunted House

Porch Roof

Cut 2

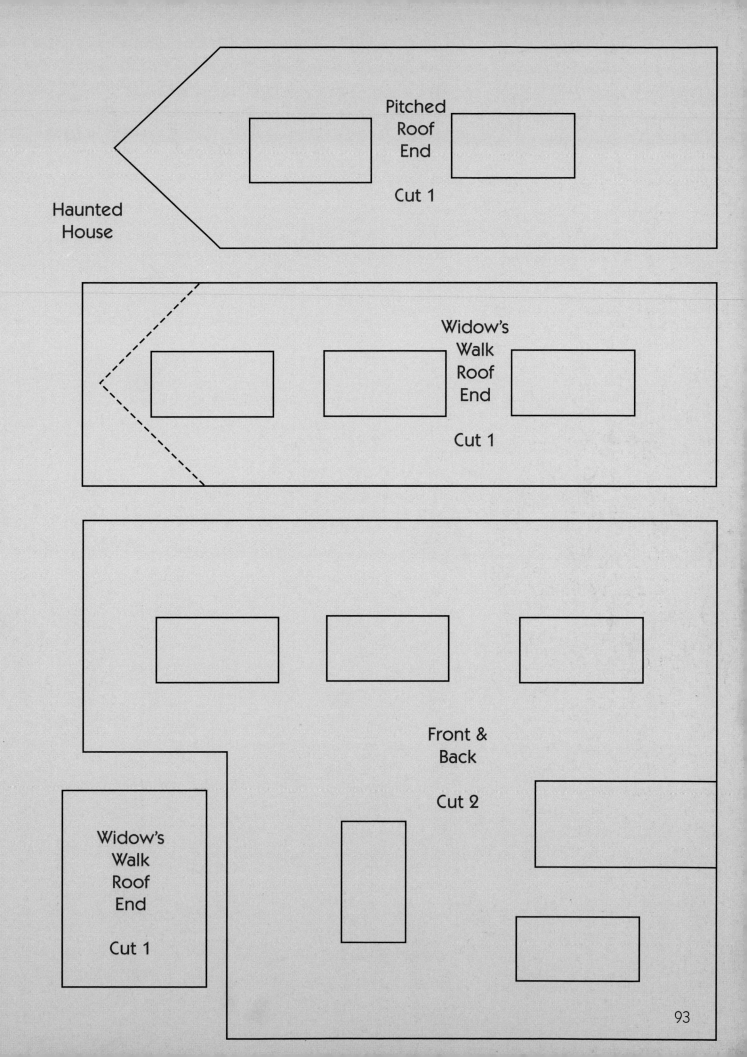

Haunted
House

Pitched
Roof
End

Cut 1

Widow's
Walk
Roof
End

Cut 1

Front &
Back

Cut 2

Widow's
Walk
Roof
End

Cut 1

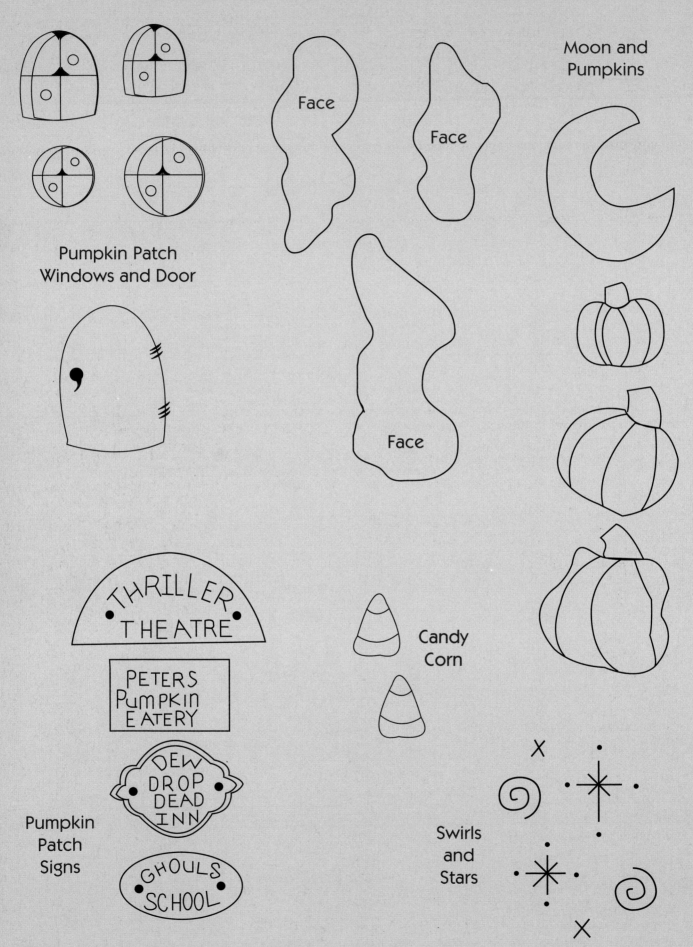

Pumpkin Patch
Windows and Door

Face

Face

Face

Moon and
Pumpkins

THRILLER
THEATRE

PETERS
Pumpkin
EATERY

DEW
DROP
DEAD
INN

Pumpkin
Patch
Signs

GHOULS
SCHOOL

Candy
Corn

Swirls
and
Stars

Metric Conversions

INCHES TO MILLIMETRES AND CENTIMETRES

INCHES	MM	CM	INCHES	CM	INCHES	CM
1/8	3	0.9	9	22.9	30	76.2
1/4	6	0.6	10	25.4	31	78.7
3/8	10	1.0	11	27.9	32	81.3
1/2	13	1.3	12	30.5	33	83.8
5/8	16	1.6	13	33.0	34	86.4
3/4	19	1.9	14	35.6	35	88.9
7/8	22	2.2	15	38.1	36	91.4
1	25	2.5	16	40.6	37	94.0
1 1/4	32	3.2	17	43.2	38	96.5
1 1/2	38	3.8	18	45.7	39	99.1
1 3/4	44	4.4	19	48.3	40	101.6
2	51	5.1	20	50.8	41	104.1
2 1/2	64	6.4	21	53.3	42	106.7
3	76	7.6	22	55.9	43	109.2
3 1/2	89	8.9	23	58.4	44	111.8
4	102	10.2	24	61.0	45	114.3
4 1/2	114	11.4	25	63.5	46	116.8
5	127	12.7	26	66.0	47	119.4
6	152	15.2	27	68.6	48	121.9
7	178	17.8	28	71.1	49	124.5
8	203	20.3	29	73.7	50	127.0

YARDS TO METRES

YARDS	METRES	YARDS	METRES	YARDS	METRES	YARDS	METRES	YARDS	METRES
1/8	0.11	2 1/8	1.94	4 1/8	3.77	6 1/8	5.60	8 1/8	7.43
1/4	0.23	2 1/4	2.06	4 1/4	3.89	6 1/4	5.72	8 1/4	7.54
3/8	0.34	2 3/8	2.17	4 3/8	4.00	6 3/8	5.83	8 3/8	7.66
1/2	0.46	2 1/2	2.29	4 1/2	4.11	6 1/2	5.94	8 1/2	7.77
5/8	0.57	2 5/8	2.40	4 5/8	4.23	6 5/8	6.06	8 5/8	7.89
3/4	0.69	2 3/4	2.51	4 3/4	4.34	6 3/4	6.17	8 3/4	8.00
7/8	0.80	2 7/8	2.63	4 7/8	4.46	6 7/8	6.29	8 7/8	8.12
1	0.91	3	2.74	5	4.57	7	6.40	9	8.23
1 1/8	1.03	3 1/8	2.86	5 1/8	4.69	7 1/8	6.52	9 1/8	8.34
1 1/4	1.14	3 1/4	2.97	5 1/4	4.80	7 1/4	6.63	9 1/4	8.46
1 3/8	1.26	3 3/8	3.09	5 3/8	4.91	7 3/8	6.74	9 3/8	8.57
1 1/2	1.37	3 1/2	3.20	5 1/2	5.03	7 1/2	6.86	9 1/2	8.69
1 5/8	1.49	3 5/8	3.31	5 5/8	5.14	7 5/8	6.97	9 5/8	8.80
1 3/4	1.60	3 3/4	3.43	5 3/4	5.26	7 3/4	7.09	9 3/4	8.92
1 7/8	1.71	3 7/8	3.54	5 7/8	5.37	7 7/8	7.20	9 7/8	9.03
2	1.83	4	3.66	6	5.49	8	7.32	10	9.14

Index